Successful Christianity
And
Basic Ministries

'Dipo Toby Alakija

ISBN: 978 - 978- 49874-6-2
ISBN: 978-49874-6-5

Printed in United States
First published in 2012 and republished in 2016 By
The Publishing House Of

CALVARY ROCK RESOURCES

19, Ajina Street, Ikenne Remo,
Ogun State,
Nigeria.

36, Thomson road
Gorton
Manchester
M18 7QQ
United Kingdom

270 Madison Avenue
Suite 1500, New York, NY 10016
United States

www.calvaryrock.org

PRACTICE OF CHRISTIANITY

(BOOK ONE)

THE SUPREME GOD

Some years ago, there was an atheist who stood on a soap-box at Hyde Park Corner, London, pouring scorn on Christian faith. He said, *"people tell me about God that exists but I can't see Him. People tell me there is life after death; but I can't see it. People tell me that there is a judgment to come, but I can't see it. People tell me there is heaven and hell; but I can't see them."* He won a cheap applause. A blind man struggled and managed to get to the soap-box to share his view too. He said, "people tell me that there is green grass all around, but I can't see it. People tell me that there is blue sky above, but I can't see it. People tell me there are trees nearby, but I can't see it. You see, I'm blind." The blind man was able to prove it to the atheist that just because he does not believe there is God does not mean He does not exist.

There are so many people who doubt the existence of God and yet they enjoy His works. Imagine how the world came into being - the mountains, the ocean, the beautiful flowers, the stars, the solar system and all you can perceive with any of your senses of perceptions. No doubt, you will come to the conclusion that there is a creative power behind the creations. The creator is God. In the book of Isaiah 43:10, the Bible says, *"you are my witnesses, saith the Lord, and My servant whom I have chosen; that you may know and believe me, and understand that I am he: before me there was no God formed, neither shall there be after me."*

We know there is God through the things He had created, through our conscience and through His words in the Bible.

There is a tract that was published some years ago by Grace and Truth. It is titled, "Challenge By An Atheist," which I cannot help but to use as the testimony to establish the fact that there is God:

He cried out boldly to the crowd: "there is no answer to prayer! It's only your imagination! Use your common sense! And there's no here after either! When we die, we're done for!"

A large crowd gathered in the town square to listen as this arrogant atheist questioned the existence of God and the value of prayer. He ended the speech by challenging anyone to debate him.

Instantly, a man in the crowd accepted the challenge, coming forward. The people eagerly made way for him, anticipating a good debate. The challenger was well dressed, but did not look like a match for the skeptic. He looked over the crowd for a moment before speaking, "I'm not a public speaker. I did not intend to dispute anything this man has said. But when he said there is no value in prayer, and challenged anyone to prove him wrong, I had to come forward."

The crowd cheered. "You see standing before you is a man who was once as big a liar, drunk, gambler and wife beater as you could find in this city. I was all these and more! My wife and daughter dreaded the sound of my footsteps. And yet, bad as I was, and unknown to me, my wife prayed for me for years and even taught my child to pray for me.

"One night, quite by accident, I ended up at home sober and much earlier than usual. When I opened the door, I could hear my little daughter, praying, 'Dear Lord, save my Daddy! Please, save my Daddy!' As she prayed her child-like prayer, I heard my wife in the background sobbing, 'Lord Jesus, please, answer her prayer.'

"I left the house quietly with strange feelings. My daughter's prayer was ringing in my ears. Did that child really care that much for me? Why? She has never known a father's love. I don't think I have ever kissed her. I got a lump in my throat and tears filled my eyes. I cried, 'Lord, help me! Lord, answer my daughter's prayer.'"

He paused and then asked his listeners, "Friends, wouldn't I be a coward if I kept silent today? How can I do anything but believe that there is a God, and that he not only hears but also answers prayers?" The debate was over. The atheist was speechless as the crowd silently went away.

Robert A Laidlaw said, proving the existence of God, '...(if) we stand together on the wharf as a big ocean liner draws alongside, and I say to you, "A lot of people think that ship is the result of someone's carefully designed plans, but I know better. There was really no intelligence at work on it at all; the iron, by some mysterious process, gradually came out of the ground and fashioned itself into plates; slowly holes were formed in the edges of these plates, and rivets appeared, flattened themselves out on either side, and after a long time, by this same evolutionary process, the engines were in place. Then one day some men on the seashore found her floating quietly in a sheltered cove." You would probably consider me a lunatic and move further into the crowd to escape my senseless chatter. Why, you know that where there is a design there must be a designer....'

Now we know there is a Supreme God, let us see a few things about Him.
(I)   There is no other God beside Him. (Isaiah 44:8) All other things or beings that are regarded as gods are the works of man or the force of the devil. Though Michel Eyquem de Montaigne did not

3

believe in God, he made a valid point when he said, *"man cannot make worm, yet he will make gods by the dozens."*

(II)   He is the maker of heaven and earth and all that are in them. (Genesis 1: 1-31)
(III)   His presence is felt everywhere. (Isaiah 66:1)
(IV)   He knows all things (1 John 3: 20)
(V)   He is all powerful. He has no beginning and no end like a wedding ring. (1 Chronicles 29:11)
(VI) He is infinitely Holy. (1 Samuel 2:2)
(VII) God is a Spirit. (John 4:24)
(VIII) He is a loving Father (1 John 3:1)
(IX) God is one yet has three personalities. In Matthew 3:13-17, we see the trinity at work. God, the Father spoke from heaven in respect of Jesus Christ, the Son with Holy Spirit; appearing like a dove. The baptismal formula in Matthew 28:19 forms the basis of trinity. It says, *"Go ye therefore, and teach all nations, baptizing them in the name of the Father, the Son and of the Holy Spirit."* The personalities of God are the Father who sent His Son, Jesus to redeem man. The Son is co-existent and co-eternal with the Father who took the form of man to die on behalf of man and the Holy Spirit performing an expressible important mission upon the earth (John 3:16,1 Timothy 2:5-6; John 5:17; John 15:26)

A lady asked me one question one day and expected me to be confused about the issue of trinity. She asked, "you preach about three Gods. Which one of them do you want us to believe?" I told her there is only one God just as there is one person. As a man is made up of the body, the spirit and the soul yet he is one, so is God; the Father, God the Son and God the Holy Spirit. She went further to say, "if Jesus is God, who was in control of the world when He was in the grave for three days." I replied by asking her if she believed that God is present everywhere. She said she believed. I told her if she believed, she did not need to ask me that question.

With the above things which we have learned so far about God, we can now study the practice of Christianity, especially in modern days. First, let us consider who is a Christian.

WHO IS A CHRISTIAN?

A teacher just taught the children of the qualities of Jesus Christ, saying, "He is gentle and caring. He loves everybody including children. He is good to everybody."

A child of about seven cried out involuntarily, "I know him. He lives next to our house. He is good to everybody. He loves me and I love him too." The child assumed that a Christian brother who lived near her home was Jesus because his ways of life showed he is a Christian.

In another case, a man who never claimed to be a Christian went to the Pastor of a Church that made his wife a Deaconess and said, "if my wife with her kind of attitude is a Deaconess in this Church, I think I am qualified to be the General Overseer of your denomination."

With so many instances most of which are negative, the issue of Christianity is being misrepresented by so many people around the globe. The alarming level of compromise of the Church like a gay being installed as a bishop and the worldliness of many Christians like those who do not see the need to dress decently even in the Church makes it very crucial to draw a distinction between Practical Christianity and Christianity as a form of religion.

The modern activities make it difficult to see God's role model of Christianity and man's model. Christianity is a way of life but many see it as one of the other religious activities around. Most of what we see in Christianity today is a perverted model. God's standard is still the same as it is written in Bible. Because God can never change, His words and standard remain the same even though the world have changed a lot ever since the time believers were first called Christians in Antioch.

It is important to see what Christianity is all about and why all must be Christians by practice rather than by religion.

In the book of Acts 11: 26, the Bible recalls that the disciples of Jesus Christ were first called Christians in Antioch. Like the girl that assumed that the Christian Brother that lived next to her house was Jesus Christ, there are certain attributes of the Lord which the people saw in the lifestyles of the disciples before they began to call them Christians. Christian simply means Christ-like or like Christ. In other words, for anyone to be a real Christian, he or she must be like Christ.

No one, as a matter of fact can be like Christ because of our sinful nature unless certain things take place. These things are part of what would be studied in this book. They are:

1. HEARING THE WORD:

In the book of Romans 10: 17, the Bible says, *"so then faith comes by hearing, and hearing by the word of God."* When a person hears the word of God in any way or through any means, faith that brings about salvation through Jesus Christ comes. This may not be immediate. To illustrate this, I will share the testimony of a Muslim scholar in Nigeria who became a fire brand evangelist through a tract titled: "Only one life." When this man was given the tract, he read only the title and threw it away angrily. The title began to haunt him. He kept hearing, "Only One Life" everywhere he went. He became so troubled that he went to a Christian who shared the word of God with him. It took time but the Muslim later became a fervent Christian.

It must be noted here that God gives all Christians the privilege to share His word with others even though He could use angels to do that. It is so important to share the word of God with everybody that Jesus said in Mark 16:15, *"Go ye into all the world, and preach the gospel to every creature."* When a person hears the word of God, it sinks into the spirit. When exposed to the right environment, it begins to grow like a seed as in the parable of Jesus in Luke 8:4-8.

2. BUILDING FAITH:

After hearing the word of God, according to Romans 10:17, what follows is faith in Jesus Christ.

In Hebrew 11:1, the Bible defines faith as *"...the substance of things hoped for, evidence of things not seen."*

Faith has a lot to do with relationship of man with God and the relationship with God has a lot to do with his life as a believer. Through faith, he can connect his spirit with Spirit of God; making him supernatural instead of a natural person. Faith can be built or destroyed by things a person hears, sees or perceives through his other human senses.

Without faith in God, a believer begins to think or behave or see things like unbeliever. Thus he is unable to please God. (Hebrew 11:6.)

There are two types of faith. One can be defined as the belief in Jesus Christ that brings about salvation. In Romans 10:10, the Bible says, *"For with the heart man believes unto righteousness; and with the mouth confession is made unto salvation."* This type of faith which can be called saving faith justifies a person to be a child of God according to John 1:12. A person is not made a Christian because he has good works to show or because he follows the law as the book of Galatians 2:16 explains but rather because he believes in Jesus Christ.

The second type of faith the Bible talks about is what can be described as living faith. It is one of the fruits of the Holy Spirit which a Christian must exhibit according to Galatians 5:22-23. This type of faith comes after new birth. Living faith brings about manifestations of physical and spiritual works. The Bible says in James 2:17, *"Even so faith, if it has not works, is dead being alone."*

I would like to use the illustration of the people swimming in a sea that is full of violent tides to describe the two types of faith the Bible talks about.

The sea tides are sweeping the people through a tunnel that leads to a lake of fire. The people always struggle in vain to get out of the ocean. Then a man with long hands that can reach out to everyone came to rescue them. He stretched out his hands to as many as are willing to accept his offer to help them, not because any of them deserve to live but because he loves them. Many people held the hands but they do not put enough efforts to hang on until they reach the shore. Such people fall back into the sea and are swept by the tides through the tunnel to the lake of fire. Some did not even border to hold the hands while some are able to hold them and hang on until they reached a save place. The man with the long hand is Jesus Christ. His long hand is His Name (John 1:12). The sea is the world and sins are the tides that take people to the lake of fire called hell. The save place is heaven. Those who reject the offer are those who do not believe in the name of Jesus. The receipt of the hand by some people is the faith that brings about salvation (freedom from sins) and the efforts to hang on till the end is the living faith that brings about works.

Believers need of exercise these two types of faith if they really want to get to the kingdom of God. The saving faith is what brings about new birth while the living faith is what keeps him alive spiritually until he meets the Lord.

3. NEW BIRTH:

In John 3:3, the Bible says, *"Jesus answered and said unto him, verily, verily, I say unto thee, except a man be born again, he cannot see the kingdom of God."*

New birth is the greatest of all miracles and the most remarkable mystery on earth. It is as a result of new birth that the sinful nature of a man is overcome through the power of the Holy Spirit. A man who is doomed for eternal destruction can get to the kingdom of God after new birth. The mystery of new birth can be traced to the issue of the first and the last Adams. The first Adam was made a living soul through the breath of God after his flesh was made from dust. (Genesis 2:7) and the last Adam is a life giving Spirit. In 1 Corinthians 15:45, the Bible says, *"And so it is written, the first man Adam was made a living soul; the last Adam (Jesus) was made a life giving Spirit."* Every human

7

being - both dead and alive are from the first man Adam. Because the flesh of Adam was made corruptible (sinful) the day he ate the forbidden fruit, all human beings by nature and practice become sinners. Another Adam was therefore needed to bring man back to his original position in the plan of God. This can only be done by having the nature of God. Since no one on earth or in heaven possesses this nature, Jesus who is God, according to John 1: 1-5, has to come to impact the nature of God into man through faith (saving faith) in Him and faith (living faith through works and ways of life) by obeying His Words.

In 1 Peter 1:23, the bible says, *"Being born-again not of corruptible seeds but of incorruptible by the word of God, which lives and abided for ever."* In other words, there are two types of seeds from the two Adams. The one that is corruptible is the seed of the first man, Adam through flesh. The incorruptible seed is the eternal life in Jesus Christ. Only belief in Him and obedience to the word of God can bring about the new life in a person. When a person receives this life, he becomes a new person entirely. Then he can be said that he is born-again. The corruptible seed of the first Adam is replaced with incorruptible seed of the second Adam (Jesus) through the Word of God.

4. HOLY SPIRIT BAPTISM:

John, the Baptist while talking about Jesus said in Matthew 3:11 *"I indeed baptize you with water unto repentance: but he that cometh after me is mightier than I, whose shoes I am not worthy to bear: he shall baptize you with the Holy Ghost, and with fire..'* Here we can see two types of baptism - Water Baptism and Holy Spirit Baptism. The emphasis is on Holy Spirit Baptism though Water Baptism is required because of its importance. Apart from the example Jesus laid down when he was baptized by immersion, He said in Mark 16:15-16, *"Go ye into all the world, and preach the gospel to every creature. He that believeth and is baptized shall be saved; but he that believeth not shall be damned."* In other words, everybody that is save must be baptized by immersion, which signifies that the person is dead to the flesh, buried and resurrected just as Jesus died and resurrected.(Colossians 2:12)

Holy Spirit baptism is the dwelling of Holy Spirit inside a Christian.

Jesus knows the importance of baptism of Holy Sprit in the life of Christians. That is why He said in the book of Acts of the Apostles 1:8, *"But you shall receive power, after the Holy Spirit has come upon you: and you shall be my witnesses in Jerusalem, and in all Judea, and in*

Samaria, and unto the uttermost part of the earth."

Holy Spirit is God as pointed earlier because He is the personality of God. The word trinity means three in one or one person manifesting in three personalities.

God created the world through His Word. Jesus is the Word that created the world, according to John 1:1-3 which says, *"In the beginning was the Word, and the Word was with God, and the Word was God. The same was in the beginning with God. All things were made by Him; and without Him was not any thing that was made."*

When man fell from the position of dominion of all God had created after eating the forbidden fruit, there was no one to restore him. Seeing no one to redeem man from sin, the Word of God had to come out from God and entered the womb of Virgin Mary to become flesh according to John 1:13-14. Mary gave birth to Jesus who came as the Redeemer of mankind. He went back to God and pours out His Spirit on those who believe in Him. The Holy Spirit manifests Himself in the lives of believers through the fruits of the Spirit that is recorded in Galatians 5:22-23. These fruits which are the attributes of Jesus Christ are what people see in the lives of His disciples in Antioch before they called them Christians for the first time.

The Holy Spirit, according to Acts 1:8, is to make Christians powerful and effective witness. These two things can be explained as follows:

(i) **Powerful Christianity:** This is the type of Christianity Jesus talked about in Matthew 11:12 when He said, *"And from the days of John the Baptist until now the kingdom of heaven suffers violence and the violent takes it by force."* This means that the passion and determination to possess the kingdom of God must be in all Christians. The passion for materialism and other things must be replaced with passion for holy living and service to God. Christians must maintain the right attitude towards everybody, everything and in all situations.

I will always remember the day I had an encounter with the Lord. So many people have told me about Jesus right from the time I was in elementary school but it never made an impact on me. One mid night, however, while I was sleeping, my spirit left my body and was taken into another world where I saw all the people that had preached to me at one time or the other. They were all testifying against me that they preached to me but I refused to yield. I became very frightened of the judgment of God. Jesus in his mercy told me He was giving me another chance. Of course, I did not need anyone to preach to me before I surrendered my life totally to Christ that day. The most wonderful thing about my conversion was that people noticed it immediately through

9

my changed attitude without me telling anyone of my conversion. This is not my work but that of the Holy Spirit.

Powerful Christianity is evidenced in the interests and lifestyle of a person. As in the case of the child who could see Jesus living in the life of a brother that lived near her house, Jesus should be seen living in the life of a Christian. It is not enough to go to Church, pray and worship God but also live by the Word of God everyday.

(ii) **_Effective witnessing_**: I want to use a story in one of my story books: Young Generation Bible Club Story Book for children to explain the need for effective witnessing. There was a man who has many children. They lived in a mansion with one another. One day, fire broke out in that house and one of the children managed to escape. He was so joyful about his escape from the fire that he did not border about the rest of the children in the house. He made little or no effort to rescue the rest in the fire. They were all burnt to death. When his father came home, he excitedly went to him and cried, "Father, I'm save from the fire!" His father looked sorrowful because he did not want to lose any of his children. The child asked him, "don't you love me?" He replied, "I do but I do not desire anyone to die. That is the reason I'm not happy."

The father is God and the child is the Christian who does nothing to save those who are heading to hell.

One of the things that a Christian would like to do immediately he becomes truly born-again is to begin to share his experience with others. He may not yet know how to pray, let alone to be familiar with the word of God but certainly; he would like to tell people about Jesus. Unknown to many people, there is power in telling people about Jesus. Satan hates people to know about Jesus because a lot of enemies are created for him through that. So he does all he can to stop people from telling others about Jesus. God always equip those who are involved in witnessing. It matters to God that people are told about Jesus because, according to Ezekiel 18:23, He does not desire anyone to die the second death that is recorded in Revelation 21:8. Holy Spirit gives Christians the boldness and power to witness.

One of the ways a Christian can grow steadily is through witnessing, sharing his Christian faith with others. Through that, he learns to be a bold Christian, apt to teach the word of God and able to work and rely on the Holy Spirit to touch those he wants to preach to.

When I gave my life to Christ, what I enjoy most is evangelism, not even prayer. My drive to see people save forced me into fasting and praying and reading the word of God so that I could have more insight into what to tell people. If a person is really fervent in witnessing, the chances are that he is being prepared for a ministry either in the Church or outside. No matter the calling of any Christian, he or she must start off with effective witnessing. I noticed the followings in effective witnessing:

(I) Christians grow steadily through telling others about Jesus Christ. A top Satanist who gave his life to Christ in Nigeria became a terror to the kingdom of hell by exposing the devil while witnessing. God gave him the enablement to be able to do that publicly. He could not graduate from the Bible school before he became a national evangelist.

(II) God often uses witnessing to prepare a Christian for the greater work ahead of him in the ministry. God does not make a minister out of a Christian without him first getting involved in effective witnessing. In fact, everybody must be involved in it. God used my drive for evangelism when I became a Christian as the foundation of my evangelistic ministry today. By the grace of God, we have produced a number of evangelical films that are being used nation wide to preach the gospel in Nigeria, apart from the books I have the privilege to write for Churches to use as teaching materials.

(III) The challenges of what to say or what to do in a particular situation often make Christians to pray and feed on the word of God.

5. FEEDING ON WORD OF GOD:

Because a person is baptized with the Holy Spirit does not mean he does not need to feed on the word of God. Thinking like that is the same as thinking that there is someone who is so strong that he can stay alive without food. As it is essential for man to eat so that he may live, feeding on the word of God is also essential for him to stay spiritually alive and healthy.

The word of God is everything to a Christian. He can easily be destroyed if he neglects the word. The word of God says in Hosea 4:6 that the people of God are destroyed for lack of knowledge. Ignorance of the word of God can lead to destruction. Hence all Christians must always feed on the word of God. The spirits of anti-Christ are always attacking the word of God in the lives of the people at various levels and places, including the Church. Ignorance of the word of God makes it possible for false ministers to replace it with human opinions. I have heard a preacher saying a life of holiness is impossible just because he cannot live it. The danger in living by what other people say is that God would not base His judgment on what people say or think but on His Word. So the opinion of man about eternity does not matter. What

11

matters is Word of God.

When a person becomes born-again, he is like a new born baby who must be fed with milk. His spiritual life must be looked after by a matured person who may be his Pastor or Bible teacher. The Bible says in 1 Peter 2:2, '*as new born babes, desire the sincere milk of the word that you may grow thereby.*'

What a believer takes immediately after new birth will determine if he will be a Christian by practice or by religion. His ways of life will show the type of Christianity in him. Although he may make mistakes as to the obedience to the word of God but what he does after the mistakes will determine if he will be back on track or back to the world.

The life of a healthy Christian will reflect the word of God because it is written in his heart and read by everybody that sees him as the second book of Corinthians 3:2 says. The word of God takes a Christian from one level of maturity in Christianity to another, adding diligences to his faith and to his calling (2 peter 1:5-6).

Christianity is more of a way of life than religion or what a person claims. The word of God is the food and the map every Christian needs before he can get to the kingdom of God.

6. FOCUS ON ETERNITY:

There is eternal life and eternal death. In John 3:16, the Bible says, '*For God so loved the world that he gave his only begotten Son, that whosoever believes in him should not perish, but have everlasting life.*' From this passage, we can see eternal life and eternal death. Eternal life is eternity in heaven while eternal death is eternity in hell. At this point, it must be noted that no matter the theology of any religion; heaven and hell are real. Apart from the proofs in the word of God, there are far too many evidences that prove this to be. I would like to illustrate this with the testimony of an elderly man in the Church which I will never forget as long as I live.

The elderly man was fervent and loving. It was almost impossible not to love this man for his activities in the church were quite remarkable. He fell sick one day and stayed on his sick bed in the hospital for two days without eating or saying a word. We prayed for him in the Church and went to the hospital to continue the prayer. As we were praying, he suddenly opened his eyes. We were happy, thinking he has received his healing. He said, 'please, don't pray for me again. I've met Jesus in heaven. He said your prayer was holding him from taking me away from this world. He said if I really want to come home, I should tell you to let me go.' Then one of us said, 'we don't want you to go.' Tears dropped from his eyes as he said, 'if you really love me and if you know how beautiful heaven is, you would let me go.' At last and at least, we resolved to let the will of the Lord be done. The elderly man died that day.

Since Jesus is life, He is the giver of eternal life. Without Him, no one can have eternal life. In John 14:6, the Bible says, '*Jesus said unto him, I am the way, the truth, the life: no man comes unto the Father, but by me.*' When a person gives his life to Jesus Christ, he becomes a new person through the process of new birth. He becomes a member of royal priesthood and a peculiar person, according to 1 Peter 2:9. Through obedience to the word of God, he becomes a citizen of heaven.

Things that guarantee eternal life in heaven are:
(I) New birth (John 3:3)
(ii) Holiness (Ephesians 4:22-24)
(iii) Obedience to the word of God (Hebrew 3: 12-15)

Price for the kingdom of God: The kingdom of God is called heaven. It is a place of eternal rest for those who are born-again. It is also the place God stays according to Psalm 53:2 and the inheritance of all believers according to John 14:1-3 which says, '*Let not your heart be troubled: you believe in God, believe also in me. In my Father's house are many mansions: if it were not so, I would have told you. I go to prepare a place for you. And if I go and prepare a place for you, I will come again, and receive you unto myself: that where I am, there ye may be also.*'

The followings are what can cause Christians to miss God's kingdom:
(I) Sin. (Romans 6: 23)
(II) Disobedience to God (1 Samuel 15:23)
(III) Ungodly friends (2 Corinthians 6:14, Ephesians 5:11, 1 Corinthians 15:33)
(IV) Ignorance of the word of God (Hosea 4:6)

Eternal Life: is life that has no end. It last forever in heaven. No one can live forever in the mortal body. In 1 Thessalonians 4:13-14, the Bible says: '*But I would not have you to be ignorant, brethren, concerning them which are asleep, that ye sorrow not, even as others which have no hope. For if we believe that Jesus died and rose again, even, so them also which sleep in Jesus will God bring with him.*' 1 Philippians 1:21 says, '*For to me to live is Christ, and to die is a gain.*'

From the above passages, we can see that death is like changing a place of residence. The mortal body is like a cloth which the real man (the soul) puts on. That is why the Bible refers to man as soul in Ezekiel 18:20 which says, *'The soul that sins, it shall die…'* When the soul is stripped of the body, he or she dies a physical death. That is when eternal life or death begins. You can study more about deaths in this course book on Deliverance but what is instructive to note here is that eternal life begins is heaven while eternal death begins in hell.

The Bible says in Revelation 21:3-4, *'And I heard a great voice out of heaven saying, Behold, the tabernacle of God is with men, and he will dwell with them, and they shall be their God. And God shall wipe away all tears from their eyes: and there shall be no more death, neither sorrow, nor crying, neither shall there be any more pain for the former things are passed away.'* Eternal life had been made available for us through the shedding of the blood of Jesus but many do not get it even though they desire it. The reason is found in Romans 14:17, which says, *'For the kingdom of God is not meat and drink; but righteousness, and peace, and joy in the Holy Ghost.'* Eternal life is free but it takes grace to keep it because a lot of sacrifices are needed to maintain it. It is like a poor man who is given a priceless car. He can get so many benefits through the car but it requires a lot to maintain it. The kingdom of God where eternal life begins is not meat and drink as the Bible says but righteousness. The Bible says something about living a righteous life which makes people forgo eternal life in 2 Timothy 3:12. It says, *'Yea, and all that will live godly in Christ Jesus shall suffer persecution.'*

Persecutions have taken various shapes in modern days. Let us first see the Biblical meaning of persecution in 2 Corinthians 4:8-10. The passage says, *'we are troubled on every side, yet not distressed; we are perplexed, but not in despair; persecuted, but not forsaken; cast down, but not destroyed; Always bearing about the body the dying of the Lord Jesus, that the life also of Jesus might be made manifest in our body.'*

Persecution can be generally described as any thing that troubles a Christian or makes him distressed or perplexed or feel physically or mentally persecuted or forsaken as a result of his faith in Christ. To illustrate this, I will love to share with you the story of a Christian who was a soldier. He was in the train with other soldiers, reading his Bible. One of the soldiers snatched the Bible from him and threw it away through the window. Then he and others went ahead to make fun of him for his faith in Christ. He did not allow this to border him. So he prayed to God to forgive them. Few days later, the Bible was posted to him by a man who found and read it. He found the name and address of

14

the soldier on the Bible and sent it to him, telling him how he found the Lord when he read it.

Some reasons God allows persecution include: making the Christians to grow strong, to manifest Himself in the midst of persecutions, to give room for His word to spread as in the case in Acts 8:1-25 and to give them the chance to prove if they are really ready to stand by Him all the time.

This reminds me of what happened in a communist country many years ago when and where Christians are being seriously persecuted for their faith. Some communist soldiers burst into a church, tore off the poster of Jesus Christ and told the Church leaders to deny Christ by spitting on the poster if they wanted to stay alive. Three of the leaders spat on the poster. A little girl came out from among the congregation and went to clean off the spit. She told the soldier to kill her if they wished. The soldiers took the little girl and the three Church leaders out of the church. The rest in the church heard three gun shots and later brought the girl back to the church. One of the soldiers said they loved people who were ready to die for what they believed even when faced with threat of death. That was why the girl was spared while the three leaders were shot dead. That incident made the church ready to die for their faith. We cannot possibly exhaust every thing about persecution but there is need to see persecution in the modern days as what makes Christians stronger. It is observed that people are always made stronger Christians when they are persecuted than when they are not.

Persecutions in the modern days come in various ways but the brain behind it is the devil. He uses people and circumstances as means to persecute Christians. His primary aim is to steal people of God, kill them spiritually and bring about their eternal death as John 10:10 says. Persecution may be physical or mental. In the modern days, mental persecution is very common. The good news is that a Christian may choose not to be persecuted mentally if he focuses his mind on things above. He will be persecuting himself if he thinks of what he would have gained if he had not been a Christian. There are so many things around us that demand that we compromise with our faith but we have to think of what Jesus said in Luke 9:25, *'For what is a man profited if he gain the whole world, and lose himself, or suffer loss?'* To start with, nobody can gain the whole world. Even if he gains the whole world, Jesus asks of his gain if he loses his soul. A pastor asked the people that were gathered during the burial ceremony of a wealthy man, 'who loves this man most?' His wife claimed to be the one. The pastor asked her to kiss him if she really loved him. Everybody was startled. The woman said it was not possible. Apparently the pastor meant to prove it that human love is limited. Since the man was dead, he has been separated from all he has; including his family. He was now left to face eternal life or eternal torment.

Eternal Torment: This is also called eternal or second death. In Revelation 21:8, the Bible says, *'But the fearful, and unbelieving, and the abominable, and murderer, and whoremonger, and sorcerers, and idolaters, and all liars, shall have their parts in the lake which burns with fire and brimstone: which is the second death.'*

If people are conscious of eternal death, there will be little work for Christians to do but, despite human knowledge; advanced technology and so-called philosophies, the world is still very ignorant of eternal death. I gave a documentary film about a dead man that came back to life to a wealthy man. He gave his life to Christ after watching it because it was full of truth about eternity. I gave the same film to another person who said it was just a film. What I told him is what I use to tell every skeptic I met. What if you think hell and heaven are not real and it turns out to be real when you die, what are you going to do? I want to take little time to explain eternal death. Now the first question to ask is: what is eternal death?

The Bible says in John 11:25 and 26, *'Jesus said unto her, I am the resurrection and the life: he that believeth in me, though he were dead, yet shall he live. And whosoever lives and believes in me shall never die. Do you believe this?'*

The above passage distinguishes physical life from eternal life and physical death from eternal death.

Physical death is the changing from mortal body into immortal one. To any Christian who goes through this kind of death, the Bible says in 1 Thessalonians 4:14 that it is sleep in the Lord. Also in Philippians 3:20-21, the Bible says, *'For our citizenship is in heaven; from which also we look for the Saviour, the Lord Jesus Christ: who shall change our humble body, that it may be fashioned like unto his glorious body, according to the working where by which he is able even to subdue all things unto himself.'*

Eternal death takes place if a person dies a physical death without accepting Jesus Christ as his Lord and Saviour. Ezekiel 18:4 says, *'Behold, all souls are mine; as the soul of the father, so also the soul of the son is mine: the soul that sins, it shall die.'* The death indicated here is not the death of physical body but that of the soul. Only eternal death can get the soul.

Eternal death which is the second death is explained in the book of

Revelation 21:8 which says, '*But the fearful, and unbelieving and sorcerers and idolater and all liars shall have their part in the lake which burns with fire and brimstone: which is the second death.'* Eternal death, therefore, is the presence of a person in the lake of fire called hell. I pray that God will guide you to heaven so that you do not end up there. Amen.

CHRISTIAN POTENTIALS

(BOOK TWO)

INTRODUCTION

To understand what this course titled Christian potentials is all about, there is need to consider the potentials of a seed. Late Myles Maroe gives a perfect description of a seed by saying that if he holds the seed of a tree in his hand, he is actually holding a forest. So it is a wrong notion to say a tree cannot make a forest. As far as God is concerned, even a seed will make a forest because it has the potentials to produce a tree and a tree will produce more seeds that can make more trees that can produce a forest. In Genesis chapter 7, the Bible makes us to understand how God preserved the lives of the living things in Noah's ark. God did not create another animals and people when He destroyed the world during the time of Noah. It was the pairs of those living things that reproduced themselves before we have them in billions.

The same principle is applicable to Christian potentials. At this stage, we may ask. What is Christian potentials in this context?

Christian potentials may be simply defined as the total sum of the abilities in a genuine believer to make exploit for Christ according to the grace given to him or her. It must be understood here that no matter how great the vision or dream God gives to a Christian, he has the potentials to carry it out. It may seem impossible to carry it out but the vision given by God cannot be frustrated. God-given vision is like the word that is sent by God to accomplish a task. The word or vision cannot go back to God without result. Once God gives the vision, it can be considered done because God has given to the person with vision the potentials to carry it out. Someone said that God's vision cannot lack God's provision. As a matter of rigid principle, all Christians have certain potentials deposited inside them to carry out certain tasks that are peculiar to them. This potential is to glorify the name of the Lord in the work of the ministry and to carry it out whether alone or with other people who are ordained by God. That is the reason this course is of great importance. It will help you identify your potential and how to make the best use of it to the gory of God.

SOME OF THE THINGS THE BIBLE COMPARES
A CHRISTIAN WITH

The Bible compares a Christian with a good number of things but we shall consider just four of them. These four things will help to identify the potentials in a Christian. They are: (1) A seed (2) A branch of a tree

19

(3) A sheep and (4) A treasure.

By comparing Christians with these things, the Bible makes it clear that the most important thing for them to do before they begin to realize their potentials is to seek first the kingdom of God and His righteousness as Matthew 6:33 says. When other things are given to them, according to that passage, they must learn to invest their treasures in heaven and not on earth as Matthew 6:19-21 says. The followings are the basic ways Christians must invest their treasures:

(I) By paying their tithes and offerings from their income, according to Malachi 3:8-12, they are keeping treasures in heaven.

(II) By sharing what they have with needy people, they are also keeping their treasures in heaven (Matthew 25:34-46)

(III) When they spend their time ministering to the physical and spiritual needs of other people, they are also investing into the kingdom of God.

A SEED

In 1 Peter 1:23-25, the word of God says, *"Being born again, not of corruptible seed but of incorruptible, by the word of God, which lives and abides for ever. For all flesh is as grass, and all the glory of man as the flower of grass. The grass withers, and the flower therefore falls away: But the word of the Lord endures forever. And this is the word which by the Gospel is preached unto you."*

A Christian may be compared with a seed which has certain potentials. He may not know himself or the potentials in him unless God reveals it to him just as one may not know the seed of mustard if he has not seen one before. The only way to know the kind of seed one has is to subject it to the right environment. Of course, certain process will have to take place before the seed begins to realize its full potentials. As it is in the seed which must first be buried and dead in the ground before it begins to grow, a Christian must also be dead to sin and buried with Jesus Christ by water baptism before he begins to realize his full potentials. In Romans 6: 6-8, the bible says, *"Knowing this, that our old man is crucified with Him, that the body of sin might be destroyed, that henceforth we should not serve sin. For he that is dead is free from sin. Now if we be dead with Christ, we believe that we shall also live with Him."* It is after the person is dead to the flesh that his potential will begin to manifest. If he is not dead to the flesh, the potential will be dormant. The Bible says in Colossians 3:3, *"For you are dead, and your life is hid with Christ in God."*

After becoming dead to the flesh, the Christian must be constantly watered with the word of God the way a seed is watered before it begins to grow. The Bible says in 1 Peter 2:2, *"As new born babes, desire the pure milk of the word, that you may grow thereby."* As he receives the water, the light of the Holy Spirit will radiate in his spirit every time and causes him to be nurtured, depending on the amount of the word he takes. A Christian tends to grow as he drinks of the living water in the word.

If you have been to a river, you will discover that the plants around the place are always well nourished. They are always green. If you have been to a dry land where rains hardly fall, you will see even trees becoming withered for lack of water. It is the same with a Christian who meditate on the word of God and the one who hardly read it. If he does not read the word of God, he is likely to dry up spiritually within a very short time. If he feeds on the word constantly, he will grow.

As small as a seed is, it has the potentials to grow into the tap and other roots, the trunk, the branches, the leaves and the fruits, bringing forth more seeds. The same is applicable to a Christian. A Christian has the potentials to establish a ministry that can win millions of souls or establish an organization that is big enough to yield much more than he can dream of. Although one may find it difficult to imagine a big tree emerging from a small seed yet it can yield much more trees than any one can imagine.

We all must know, however, that as there are differences in the potentials of all the seeds, there are also different potentials in Christians. The potential in the seed of an apple will bring about an apple tree and the seed of a mango will bring about a mango tree. We are all endowed with different potentials according to our abilities or what you can call stamina. Stamina in this context implies the emotional, physical and spiritual maturity. To illustrate this, I want you to think of various sizes of fishes that you know. There are some that are so big that they can only be found in an ocean. Some can be found in the river while some can be kept in aquariums. All these fishes grow according to their potentials or abilities. The ministries of a Christian likewise grow into various sizes, according to the abilities and grace given to him. So a Christian must not venture into the ministries or what he knows he has no ability to perform.

The other thing a Christian is compared with is a branch of a tree (Vine).

A BRANCH OF A TREE

In the book of John chapter 15:1 to 8, Jesus made us realized that

He is the Vine (tree) and Christians are the branches. If a branch is separated from the tree, it will die. The reason is that all the sources of nourishment and life are from the tree which is deep rooted into the ground. For the branch to stay alive, it must abide in the tree because it cannot function on its own. A Christian must abide in Christ if he has to maintain his eternal or spiritual life.

Apart from that, for a Christian to produce fruits in which seeds (those who are spiritual babies or those who are yet to come to the knowledge of Christ) are embodied, he must abide in Christ. Note here that it is possible for a Christian to think he abides in Christ and still refuses to bear fruits. In John 15: 2, Jesus said, *"every branch in me bears not fruit he takes away: and every branch that bears fruit, he prunes it, that it may bring forth more fruit."*

Many Christians are not bearing fruits due to any of the following reasons that are explained in the parable of the sower in Matthew 13:3-8.

1. They do not understand the word of life that is supposed to bring fruits into their lives. Therefore they are taken away. (Matthew 13:19)
2. They do not have roots in Christ who is the Vine to keep the word of life. When problems or tribulation or persecution arise, they give up the seed of life. (Matthew 13: 21)
3. Others that refuse to bear fruits are the ones that are choked because of the care of this world and deceitfulness of riches. (Matthew 13: 22)

Everything a branch (a Christian) needs to bear fruits even in his old age is right in the Vine (Jesus). Jesus has made available all the things a Christian needs to realize his potentials (to be fruitful). He does not need to go and search for them. They are embodied right in Christ.

The things a Christian would need which he would find in Jesus before he begins to bear fruits are Holy Spirit, Gift/natural Talents and The Word Of God:

(A) **_Holy Spirit_:** In Act 1:8, Christians are promised Holy Spirit from Whom they shall receive power which will enable them to preach the Gospel and to perform supernatural things. Christians are the people having the greatest potentials because the Holy Spirit enables them to go beyond their natural abilities and limitation of man.

To explain this, let us study the case of a woman who graduated from the University and started working as a civil servant in Nigeria. After working for a few years, she began to feel restless about the job. She felt that by then she was supposed to be a blessing to so many ministries by giving to them. Instead, she was living a life of mediocrity, doing routine job that never allowed her to exercise her skill in marketing. The Holy Spirit prompted her to resign her appointment as a civil servant. She began to sell food stuff. To so many people who knew her position in the civil service, it seemed foolish if not crazy but the Holy Spirit continued to assure her that she was doing the right thing. At last, after a few years, she was able to acquire so much experience and information about African food that it was a lot easy for her to get registered as one of the people that will be exporting Nigeria food stuff overseas. Today, the woman is a great financial blessing to many ministries in Nigeria just as she desired. If not for the Holy Spirit that urged her to continue when things were tough, she would have given up just like anyone who has no Holy Spirit to guide him or her. Apart from this, it is the Holy Spirit that helps a Christian to see the way out of difficulty which no human eye or senses can perceive.

Through the power of the Holy Spirit, a Christian can command a thing to be done and it shall be done supernaturally (Luke 11: 9-13) as pointed out. Christians have the greatest authority and potentials on earth because they have their source from God Who is not only all knowing, all powerful but also present everywhere. Through the Holy Spirit, Christians can be inspired, encouraged and strengthened when things look as if they would not work out as they hope. Unlike Satanists who get ideas from the devil, most of which are very destructive to mankind, Christians have the privileges to get uncommon ideas that will benefit humanity through inspiration of God. Christians without the Holy Spirit can never tap into the power of God and therefore will not produce any fruits.

Also embodied in the Holy Spirit Himself are fruits of the Spirit which are love, joy, peace, longsuffering, gentleness, goodness, faith, meekness and temperance as recorded in Galatians 5: 22-23. These fruits of the Spirit are attributes that are exhibited by the Christian who is filled with the Holy Spirit.

For a Christian to bear fruits, he must be alive in the Spirit and for him to be alive in the Spirit, he must be filled with Holy Spirit. Any branch that does not produce, according to John 15: 2- 6, is taken away and cast into fire (Hell)

No matter who you are or what your background may be, no matter your age or level of education; once the Holy Spirit fill you, you would do exploit. Peter who was an ordinary fisherman became a great tool that confounded the wise when the Holy Spirit filled him. Remember that the same Peter denied Jesus Christ three times in Luke 22: 55- 60. Why? It is because he had no Holy Spirit that will make him bold. Peter who denied Christ three times now stood up in the public and boldly witnessed to the people because by then he was filled with the Holy Spirit.

The Holy Spirit helps a Christian to successfully take the steps which ordinary people cannot take.

There are also gifts of the Spirit which are part of the potentials of a Christian as recorded in 1Corinthians 12:4-11. These are gifts but not fruits of the Spirit. God gives these gifts to individuals according to His will.

(B) *Gift/natural Talents:* Read Ephesians 4:11-12, Matthew 25:14-28. The natural talents of a Christian are not just given to him after conversion. It has been there. It is a gift of God given to him at birth. The gift may be dormant for so long if it is not used. As matter of fact, there is nobody in the world is without a gift or talent. After conversion, the Holy Spirit begins to assist a Christian in the way to use his gift. He first develops it by making him to do some certain things which will make him see that he is gifted in certain areas. Permit me to give the illustration of myself.

When I was in secondary school, I was very interested in creative writing and that used to attract people to me. I never knew that there are other gifts along with the gift of creative writing. So my major focus was to become a writer. When I later gave my life to Christ, the Lord made me get involved in children work. While dealing with the children, I discovered that I cannot handle the children without having certain gifts like acting. You know, if you have to tell children about a monkey, you have to jump or behave like a monkey to get their attention. Within three years of dealing with the children in Nigeria, I discovered that I was not just gifted in children work but also gifted and now trained in acting, story telling, song writing etc. The gift in acting was put into a test when God helped us to produce our first film titled: "The black worshippers."

The Holy Spirit helped me to develop all these gifts that were dormant simply by getting involved with children work. As we always quote, Charles Spurgeon said, *"Young men, young lady, if you become diligent in tract distribution, diligent in the Sunday school, you are likely people to be made into ministers; but if you stop and do nothing until you can do everything, you will remain useless, an impediment to the church or ministries instead of being a help to her. You have some talents entrusted to you, and something given you to do with which no one else can do. Find out, then, what your sphere is, and occupy it. Ask God to tell you what is your niche, and stand in it, occupying the place till Jesus Christ shall come and give you your reward. Use what ability you have, and use it at once. Be content and labour in your sphere even if it be small, and you will be wise."*

Virtually every Christian must do a humble thing before he discovers his potentials. If you study the parable of talents in Matthew 25:14-28, you will discover that diligence and faithfulness in using what God has given you is what can make God expand your coast. Even if you have not yet discovered your full potential, surely, there is always something you can with what you know you can do. You might not be able to write tracts but, surely, you can distribute them. You might not be given the opportunity to preach in the church, but, surely, you can clean the bench or sweep the floor. You are not likely going to realize your potential if you want to start big. The person who attempts successfully a small thing will get the opportunity to attempt a bigger thing.

One of the best ways to begin to realize your potentials is to get involved in things that look so minor. If you have the potentials to handle children, start gathering children in the neighbourhood right away and start to minister to them. If you have the potentials in ministering to people through songs, start composing songs for people in your family, neighbours, and friends and in the church. Waiting for the opportunity to be placed as children worker or a choir in the church is a complete waste of time. It is your gift that will make way for you, not whom or what you know. You do not have to advertise yourself as some do but God in His own time will place you in the position you will fully realize your potentials. Meanwhile, do whatever you can with what you have and with the little opportunity you have. And God who sees your faithfulness and diligence in secret will promote you openly.

(C) **_The Word Of God:_** The Bible says in 2 Timothy 2:15, *"Study to show yourself approved unto God, a workman that needs no to be ashamed, rightly diving the word of truth."* The word of God is another vital instrument a Christian needs to bear fruits. A Christian who does not read the word is like the branch of a tree whose source of nourishment had been seized or like the part of the body where blood no longer circulate. What would happen? He would dry up. Let us see the whole picture of the Christian who does not study the word of God in the parable of the ten virgins in book of Luke 25:1-13. In that parable, five of the ten virgins who all represent Christians were without enough oil in their lamps while the other five had enough. Now let's see what the lamp signifies in Psalm 119:105 which says *"Your word is a lamp unto my feet, and a light unto my path."* Lamp according to that passage signifies the word of God. Five of the virgins did not have enough word of God in their lives. So their light which can be attributed

25

to the power of the Holy Spirit went out even before the bridegroom (Jesus) comes. The other five are full of the word of God in their lives. So they were able to watch their steps to ensure that didn't go against any one of the words. In Psalm 119: 11, the Bible says, *"Your word have I hidden in my heart, that I might not sin against you."* People without the word of God never know when they are going wrong. They don't know where they are going and where they are coming from because their light is gone out and therefore they are in complete darkness. Even when they are told they are going wrong, they won't see it. They can even argue that they know the way very well because they have gone through the path before. Such people will interpret the word of God to suit their purposes. The truth is that they are in complete darkness. God does not need to reveal to anyone who a spiritually dead person is or not. His conduct and saying will reveal his level of maturity or how blind he is.

There is a man who was doing very well in his printing business. He was a good Christian as many people could see but God revealed it to him that he was spiritually dead. He shared what he dreamt with me. I told him there must be some hidden sins in his life, using the word of God to establish my points. The points never made an impact in him. No one knew he was deep in adultery until another woman became his second wife. Even at that level, he still believes he was a fervent Christian.

The word of God is so essential that no Christian can do anything without it. Apart from the fact that the word forms part of Christian life and a way of his life, there are times God will specifically speak to us what He wants us to do through his word. Note here that God will never tell a Christian to do anything that is contrary to the scriptures. So everything a Christian does must be confirmed by the word of God. The Bible says in 1 John 4:1, "Beloved, believe not every spirit, but test the spirits whether they are of God because many false prophets are gone out into the world.

A pastor encountered a false prophet one day. He prophesied that the pastor will die that year unless he followed him to his church for special prayers. The pastor laughed and said to the prophet, "The word of God tells me that I will live and declare His word. He also said, "no weapon that is formed against me shall prosper. Every tongue including the one that says I shall die shall be cut off in Jesus' Name." The prophet quickly knelt down and begged the pastor to reverse the curse.

The word of God must be the central part of the life of a Christian because God speaks to him through it. A Christian lives his life according to the word. He also shares the word of God with other people.

A SHEEP

In John 10:11-14, 26-29, Christians are compared with sheep. In Psalm 23:1, we see the Lord Jesus as our shepherd. If we study the nature of sheep, we will notice the remarkable similarity between a sheep and a Christian. As distinguished from other animals like goat, dog, wolf etc, a sheep has the followings which are the attributes of a Christian according to Ephesians 4: 1-4 (a) Meekness (b) Obedience (c) Dependence (d) Lowliness (e) Long suffering (f) Love (g) Unity. We shall be dealing with each of these attributes.

(A) **_Meekness_**: By its nature, a sheep is always meek and gentle. It is not like goat that bleats or dog that barks at everything that upsets them. They are not violent even when they are being taken to be slaughtered. I remember the time a group of butchers carelessly allowed a cow to see the knives they were about to use to slaughter it. I never knew a cow could grow so insane until that day. It went so wild that no one could come near it as it ran round the town. It really gave the people in the town a time to remember. The cow was shot eventually before it could be overcome. Christians are compared with a sheep because of its meekness. Meekness is part of the fruits of the Spirit which a Christian exhibits according to Galatians 5:22-23. Jesus who is our model was so meek that he never complained when he was taken as a lamb for the sacrifice of our sins.

(B) **_Obedience_**: this means subjecting to authority. A sheep can easily be guided to any place because of their obedient nature. In Romans 13:1-2, the Bible says, _"Let every soul be subject unto higher powers. For there is no power but of God: the powers that be ordained of God. Whoever resists the power, resist the ordinance of God: and they that resist shall receive to themselves judgment."_ Also in Hebrew 13:17, the word of God says, _"Obey them that rule over you, and submit yourselves: for they watch for your souls, as they that must give account, that they may do it with joy, and not with grief: for that is unprofitable for you."_

A sheep always obey the shepherd in all circumstances. Sometimes, the shepherd has to use rod and staff according to Psalm 23:4 which might come in form of trouble or affliction to direct or to get the attention of the sheep. At the end of it all, the sheep would obey the instruction of the shepherd. Christians need to obey God in all things

27

and in all situations if they must realize their full potentials. The obedience of a Christian can best be tested when he finds himself in a stormy situation. Generally speaking, everybody would love to obey God because we are not created to be rebellious. It is the devil who caused Adam and Eve to eat the forbidden fruit that makes man rebellious.

In Psalm 23:4, the Bible says, *"...Your rod and your staff they comfort me."* Nobody can be comforted when he is beaten with a rod or staff unless he is an obedient Christian. Rod and staff are painful when they are used to correct or direct. The rod and the staff signify terrible situation and problems as pointed earlier. When a Christian is in terrible situation and he is still willing to obey, then he is obedient. Surely, such Christian is likely to realize his full potentials. But it is a pity that there are few Christians like that. When small problems come, they begin to grumble like the people of Israel who did not expect what they found in the wilderness. The Israelites thought that within forty days, Moses will get them to the Promised Land so they were willing to obey God by leaving the land of Egypt. But what happened when they did not get what they bargained for immediately? They began to grumble about their condition, contemplating going back to Egypt.

By the nature of sheep, she doesn't complain of her condition even though she would love a change if the situation is so bad. An animal like a goat will do everything including making a lot of noise to get immediate change.

(C) **Dependence:** A sheep is so dependent on the shepherd that it can easily get lost without him. In Psalm 23:3, the Bible says, *"He restores my soul: he leads me in the paths of righteousness for his name's sake."* In that passage, we can see how much a Christian needs to depend on Jesus to lead him in the path of righteousness. The feelings of know it all make so many Christians failures in their endeavours, despite all the potentials God has given them to excel. No matter how gifted or talented a Christian may be, he still needs to depend on Jesus to give him all he needs and to direct him. The Bible says in Proverb 3:5, *"Trust in the LORD with all you heart; and lean not unto your own understanding."* The reason a Christian must not lean on his understanding is because what human beings perceive as real may not be real after all and what he does not perceive to be possible may be the real thing. Everything that happens in the physical realm must have been made in the spirit realm. That is why God sometimes reveal what He has done in the spirit realm to a Christian in the dream even though it may look impossible in the physical realm. To illustrate this, let us use the testimony of a man who went to India, a place that is notable for so many types of religions. The man had a dream that he prayed for a man that was born blind. The man's eyes were opened in the dream. When he got to the crusade ground, he found the blind man. He told the ushers to bring him to the platform and asked anyone who serve other gods to come forward to open his eyes, adding that he would put aside his God and serve any other god that was able to perform the miracle. Many people who serve graven images tried unsuccessfully to perform the miracle with their demonic powers. The man of God prayed just as he did in the dream and within a short time, the blind man had received his sight. Chaos took over the crusade ground.

A sheep is so dependent that he needs the shepherd to save him from he that is a hireling (John 10:12). Likewise, Christians must be dependent on the Holy Spirit if they must bear fruits and realize their potentials.

The story of David and Goliath in 1 Samuel 17 illustrates the dependence of the sheep on the Shepherd. David who was a boy was expected to be in the field, taking care of the sheep. One day, he was sent to his brothers on the battle field where Goliath, the giant who had been a warrior right from his youth was threatening the armies of Israel. David has learned to depend on God in all his endeavours and in frightening situations. He told the king that he could fight the giant. So he was dressed in the armour of war. He told the king that he could not fight the giant with the physical weapon of war because he was conscious of the fact that the weapon of his warfare was not carnal. It is mighty through God to the pulling down of strongholds. (2 Corinthians 10:3and 4.) This was proved to be so when he took only five stones with a sling and told the giant that he had come to him in the name of the Lord. Out of the five stones, David used only one to defeat the giant who posed a serious threat to the entire nation.

If Christians will learn to depend on God in all they do, t hey will surely make exploit that will surprise people.

(D) **_Lowliness:_** In Ephesians 4:2, the Bible says, *"With all lowliness (Humility) and meekness, with longsuffering, forbearing one another in love."* Sheep by their nature do not behave highly of themselves. Likewise Christians must not think highly of themselves or think they are better than or superior to the others because they are not. In Philippians 2:3, the Bible says, *"Let nothing be done through strife or vain glory; but in lowliness of mind let each esteem others better than themselves."* Christians must not do anything through strife if they want to fulfill their potentials. Many people who desire vainglory never realize their potentials. Instead they settle for little achievement when they are praised. The praise from men should encourage Christians to be more humble and reach for higher goals.

Sometime, people criticize others out of envy or sincere desire for improvement. A Christian who wants to realize his potentials should be able to distinguish destructive criticism from constructive type. Whatever the type criticism a Christian is faced with, he must learn not to be offended. If it is constructive criticism, he must be humble enough to learn from it. If it is not, he must not be discouraged or offended. Instead, he should wait for the result of his works or efforts to answer the cynics.

One of the ways my communication skill was enhanced was through the criticism of a friend of mine who majored in English language. He was very hard to impress. If he was not bordered about my choice of words in my creative writings, he would point out my weakness in economy of words. He did this on purpose to get the best out of me. His criticisms really helped me. Everybody needs to understand that criticism whether constructive or destructive have a vital role to play in realizing his potentials.

A Christian makes mistakes just like every other human being. So he must be humble enough to confess or admit it even publicly if that would make him loose his pride. Like Ralph Mahoney said, pride is a very good thing for a Christian to loose. Pride is number one enemy of anyone who wants to realize his potentials because according to Proverb 16:18 goes before a fall.

Lowliness is the attribute that will make a Christian feels he has done nothing even though people see him as an achiever. The moment that attribute is gone out of him, God will replace him with another person. Then he will begin to descend from the peak of his achievement to the lowest level where he would no longer be relevant to the people. There are some Christians God has used tremendously in the past but are no where to be found again while there are some that God continues to use up to their old age. The reason for this lies in the fact that some virtues like meekness, lowliness and other things that are necessary in Christian ministries are missing. How Christians excel in the use of his potentials depends a lot on how much virtues the word of God brings out of them.

Lowliness makes a Christian conscious of the fact that there are other people who are far better than him in whatever he is doing but the grace of God makes him whatever he is. It makes him conscious that he is given the privilege to work with God, not because he has all the experience or because he is more prayerful or because he is so spiritual or intelligent or rich. In fact, no one is worthy or capable of doing the work of God. God could send His angels who could be much more effective in performing their assignments than man but He chooses to give man the privilege to make exploit for Him.

When a Christian is aware of this, he will be humble to perform any assignment given to him, no matter how small or insignificant it may seem.

I heard a powerful testimony from a friend who pastors a Church that was notable for outstanding miracles. Each time he mounted the pulpit to preach, many people would receive healing and other miracles. In fact, there was a day he had to write down his sermon for a deacon to read to the congregation while he went to preach in another church. As the deacon read the sermon, there was yet another miracle. Many people were screaming with excitements. God opened the spiritual eyes of one of the members of the Church to see what was happening. There were angels standing behind the deacon. One day, however, an elderly woman who was an usher in the Church died and the miracle stopped. The pastor became concerned and sought for the face of the Lord. He asked the Lord what made the miracles to cease. Has he offended God in any way that made Him to take the gift of working miracles? The Lord told him that it was the elderly usher that was exercising the gift of working miracles by praying and fasting for the Church to always experience the miracles. Now that she is in heaven, there was no one to exercise the gift by specifically praying for the Church to experience miracles.

Lowliness makes a Christian to do things without caring who gets the credit. The more humble he is in using his gift or natural talents, the more God promotes him. The more God promotes him, the more relevant he will become in the Church and in the society.

(E) **_Longsuffering_**: This can also be explained as endurance, patience and tolerance combined together. Sheep are naturally patient - much more patient than most animals. Unlike goat or dog who will bleat and bark with complaint when faced with unpleasant condition, sheep can endure so many things. Most animals do quarrel but a sheep rarely do. A sheep does not have any horn like the goat because, by its nature, it does not need it because it never fights. Any sheep that fights had lost its nature as a sheep.

In Colossians 3:12-13, the Bible says, _"Put on therefore, as the elect of God, holy and beloved, compassion, kindness, humbleness of_

31

mind, meekness, longsuffering; forbearing one another, and forgiving one another, if any have a quarrel against any: even as Christ forgave you, so also do you."

Without the attribute of longsuffering, no Christian can tolerate other people for so long, no Christian can endure for so long and no Christian can be patient enough to receive the promise of God. Longsuffering has to do with the ability of a Christian to persevere in difficult situations. A Christian without this attribute will soon give up his faith in Christ.

A Christian brother lived with a group of impossible neighbours that took it as their duties to make life miserable for him. Whenever the women swept the floor, they would pack the dirt to his doorsteps. They did this to the brother on purpose but he was long suffering. The end result was that his attitude won a soul for Christ. Unknown to him, one man who was watching him went to ask him what made him so tolerant. His explanation made the man gave his life to Christ.

(F) **_Love_**: Is the most powerful of Christian attributes. The Bible says in 2 Peter 1:5-8, "And for this reason, giving all diligence, add to your faith virtue; and to virtue knowledge; And to knowledge self control; and to self control patience; and to patience godliness; And to godliness brotherly kindness; to brotherly kindness love. For if these things be in you, and abound, they make you that you shall neither be barren nor unfruitful in the knowledge of our Lord Jesus." Read 1John 2:5, 4: 7-12.

A critical study of the whole chapters in 1John emphasized on love. This is because Christianity is built on love of God for man. God so loves man that He gave His only begotten Son so that man may not perish but has everlasting life (John 3:16). He gave Christ so that there may be Christians. When you are really in love with someone like your wife or husband for instance, your love for him or her will make you do things for him or her which you cannot do for yourself. The power of love is what makes a person to sacrifice so many things for the one he loves. To illustrate this, I would like to relate what happened during the French revolution.

There was Countess during French revolution. At this time, many were arrested including Countess Lapiani and her maidservant. Both of them were imprisoned and from distress, sorrow and weeping; she fell asleep at last. By the time she awoke, she found herself alone and naked, her servant was no where to be found but had left her own clothes behind which the Countess had wear for she could not find her own clothes. After a while, the door opened and the prison guard said to her, "you can now go, your mistress, the Countess has been executed." When she was shown the death roll to confirm this, she read with tearful eyes: "Countess Lapiani EXECUTED!" Then it dawned on her that her faithful servant had given herself up voluntarily to be executed in her mistress' place.

Christian must be loving like the maidservant of the Countess if he was to maximize the use of his potentials. This is particularly vital for people in the ministries. Really the commandment to reach out to all souls was given to all Christians in Mark 16:15. To reach out to them, you must love them. Do all you can to win them for Christ. You need to spend so much time praying for them and preaching to them. In so doing, you will begin to witness a boom in the potentials God has given you.

You must realize that you cannot be effective in soul winning if you don't love God and the people with your whole heart. In all the dealings of a Christian, there must be love. If the attribute of love is missing in a Christian, his Christianity is of no physical and spiritual significance but mere religion.

(G) **_Unity_**: The Bible says in Psalm 133: 1, *"Behold, how good and pleasant it is for brethren to dwell together in unity."* As the presence of sheep anywhere symbolizes unity, Christianity is also about unity among the people that are characterized by love of God and common purpose which is to please the Lord and Saviour. Christians are much more powerful when they come together as one.

A Christian cannot realize his potentials all by himself, no matter how gifted. Some people do not know that their gifts are not meant for them but to minister to the Lord, to fellow Christians and to the world. It is when he uses the gifts or talents for God's purpose that He will to bless them. Quite unfortunately, many people use their gifts for the purpose of making money. I know a minister that will charge a lot of money before he agrees to preach in other people's church. To such people, Jesus is no longer for free but for sale.

The Bible says in Ephesians 4:3, *"Endeavouring to keep the unity of the Spirit in the bond of peace."* And verse 13, *"Till we all come in unity of faith, and of the knowledge of the Son of God, unto a perfect man, unto the measure of the stature of the fullness of Christ."*

There is power in unity. That is why the devil does not want Christians to come together as one flock. In the story of the tower of Babel in Genesis 11:1-8, we read about the people that came together as one, planning to perform what was obviously impossible to perform even for modern Christians. They wanted to build a tower whose top will reach heaven. If there were professionals at that time, they would have told them they were crazy. As I study the passage critically, I began to wonder how the people hope to build a tower that will reach heaven. But God has something to say about the seemingly crazy idea in verse 6. *'And the Lord said, Behold, the people are one, and they have all one language and this they begin to do: and now nothing will be restrained from them, which they have imagined to do."* In other words, God said they would have succeeded with what they imagined to do because they were one. That is the power of unity operating. If all Christians in this world come together respective of their doctrines and be united by the love and the word of God which are the basis for Christianity, they will take over the control of this world from the devil. In Deuteronomy 32:30, the Bible says, *"How should one chase a thousand, and two put ten thousand to flight, except their Rock had sold them, and the LORD had given them up?"* The question a true Christian should ask himself is, "how can God give two Christians the power to put ten thousands enemies into flight when they are constantly at each other's necks, criticizing and condemning each other even in the presence of non-Christians; thereby destroying the power in unity and causing stumbling blocks to those who are yet to know the Lord?"

A TREASURE

Apart from a seed, a branch of a tree and a sheep, the other thing a Christian can be compared with is a treasure. In Psalm 139:14, the Bible says, *"I will praise you; for I am fearfully and wonderfully made: marvelous are your works; and that my soul knows well."* In other words, everybody; especially Christians; is a treasure. He is unique in his own way. Each one of us is God's masterpiece. There is no one of your type. Therefore you must not waste yourself. In 1 Peter 2:7, the Bible says, *"Unto you therefore who believe he is precious: but unto them who are disobedient, the stone which the builder rejected, the same is made the head of the corner."* According to that passage, you are a treasure if you believe in Jesus Christ. You are a treasure because it cost Jesus His precious blood to redeem you. You are a treasure because God delights in you. So whatever you do with your life matters to Him. You will give account of your life before Him. Therefore you must begin to think of investing your potentials in the Kingdom of God.

There are four principles that will be considered relating to a Christian who is considered as a treasure. They are: (a) Principle of time (b) Principle of multiplication and (c) Principle of quality.

Principle of time: In Ecclesiastes 3:1-2, the Bible says, *"To every thing there is a season, and a time to every purpose under the heaven: A time to be born, and a time to die; a time to plant, and a time to pluck up that which is planted."* In that passage, we see that there is time for everything. What you do with your time matters a lot. Because you are a treasure, you must spend time to be productive - physically and spiritually. If you are idle, you have wasted yourself for the period you're idle. You cannot rewind the time you have wasted. The Bible says in Ephesians 5:16, *"Redeeming the time, because the days are evil."* Also in Colossians 4:5, the word of God says, *"Walk in wisdom toward them that are outsiders, redeeming the time."*

God wants us to be conscious of time because our time on earth is limited. No one can afford to waste time. So anyone that wants to realize his potentials must understand how to redeem the time. The followings are the ways to begin to redeem the time:

(A) You need to learn to invest your time by doing things that will enhance your value in life e.g. learning or undergoing training in certain areas.

(B) You must plan your time. Failure to plan the time for everything can lead to an unfulfilled or wasted life.

(C) You must always evaluate all you have done for each day and see if you have wasted that day. A time will come when you will not be able to do what you once have the strength to do.

(D) You must be productive by investing your time in teaching or training others what you have learnt.

A lot of people who gave their lives to Christ at the latter part of their lives only lived to regret that they have wasted their lives by not serving Jesus. They therefore struggled to make up for the wasted time but, of course, it is not possible to redeem it. So they adopt the principle of multiplication. They concentrated on preaching and praying for the conversion of people, especially young ones who will be productive. The time they spend in preaching and praying for the conversion of such people is precious. It is a treasure that will bring fruits. What a person does with his time determines what and where he will be in the future. It will also determine if he is investing in the kingdom of God or not. Someone said, "a successful man who is the one that works while others were sleeping." It takes time to carry out a vision. It takes time to get to the top of the ladder. You take one step after the other. And with time, people who did not take notice of your struggle will see you right on top of the ladder. The Bible tells Christians in Matthew 6:19-21 to keep their treasures in heaven. Their hearts would be where their treasures are. If a person spends his time gathering the riches of the world, one day the thieves may take them from him. If that does not happen, another person will enjoy it when he dies.

There was an old man who spent all his youth days gathering money. When he became old, his children began to covet his riches. The old man promised them that no one among them will enjoy the money. So he started dishing out his properties like Father Christmas. What has he achieved with his money? He worked so hard and got money. Now that he is old, he is dishing them out. He was supposed to have trained his children with what he has made or spend the time he has spent to make money to train them. Many people do not realize that raising children in the way of the Lord is much more important to them and to God than making money. The Bible says in Proverb 29: 17 says, *"Correct your son, and he shall give you rest; yea, he shall give delight unto your soul."* If you turn the passage the other way round, as I wrote it in the children story book titled, "The Young Generation", it will read, "don't correct your son, and he shall give you trouble; yea he shall give sorrow unto your soul." A proverb also said that a man who builds a house without building his child builds what the child will later sell.

When we were children, our parents invested their treasure in terms of money, time and energy in us. Now that we are adults, what are we doing with what people had invested in us? No one can claim that nobody invested in his or her life. Our mothers would have probably gotten rid of us before we were born. The question now is: what are we doing with the investments of God and other people in our lives?

Principle Of Multiplication: While the principle of time may not be applicable to everybody, most especially those who have wasted their time when they were young; the principle of multiplication is applicable to every Christian. This principle has to do with reproduction - both physical and spiritual reproduction. There is no Christian that cannot reproduce, no matter his age. Every Christian - both young and old are capable of reproducing. In John 15:1-6, we read it in the word of God that any Christian that is compared with the branch of a tree will be cut off, withered and cast into fire (Hell) if he refuses to bear fruits. You can see how important it is to God that all Christians reproduce. In Psalm 92:12-14, the Bible says, *"The righteous shall flourish like the palm tree: he shall grow like a cedar in Lebanon. Those that are planted in the house of the LORD shall flourish in the courts of our God. They shall still bring forth fruit in old age; they shall be healthy and* *flourishing."*

Under the principle of multiplication, your children is a must for you to train in the way of the Lord because they are what God will inherit from you when you depart from this world, according to Psalm127: 3-5. You must train them in the way of the Lord so that they will be useful to God when they grow up. The word of God says in Proverb 22:6, *"Train up a child in the way he should go: and when he is old, he will not depart from it."*

There is a story of a woman who prayed to God to give her a child at the time she had reached her menopause. She promised God that if the child is a boy, he would become a pastor or an evangelist. If it was a girl, she would marry pastor or an evangelist. God heard her vow and gave her a set of twins - a boy and a girl. When these children grew up, the male said he wanted to become a pastor. She snapped at him. "What! A pastor? You want to live a wretched life of a pastor." The female met with a man who was an evangelist. She told her mother that she wanted to marry the evangelist. The mother snapped at her too, "not in this house!" The woman either thought God was unmindful or forgetful of the vow she had made. Since the children belonged to Him, He took them home in a car accident. It was then the woman came back to her senses. She realized that God cannot be taken for a ride. That is a proof that God gives and takes. The only duty we have for our children is to train them in the way of the Lord. We cannot dictate what their lives will be because we are not their maker but rather a caretaker.

The principle of multiplication is also in relation to spiritual birth and reproduction which is what is applicable to all Christians. Souls that are won to Christ go a long way to ring the bell of joy in Heaven. They too will produce souls. For this reason, the devil hates people preaching the word to others. He knows that more enemies are created for him through conversion of souls.

Andrew applied this principle when he bent a great deal of his efforts upon one person - Peter when he first met Christ. Peter who later knew Christ reproduced thousands. Andrew as a matter of fact is the grandfather of those thousands. A Christian has the potential to reproduce in thousands, no matter his age, background and profession. Unless he is spiritually dried up, he must bear fruits. The followings are the process of reproducing:

(A) Through constant prayers (1Thessalonians 5:17)
(B) Through preaching the word of God to people in whichever way he can (Mark 16:15, 2Timothy 4:5)

(C) Follow up and establishing the people in the word by giving them sound Biblical teachings (Ephesians 4:14 and 15, 2 Timothy 4:2-5) No one gives birth to a spiritual child and allow him or her to die of spiritual starvation or of diseases like heresy. (1Timothy 4: 1-3 and Ephesians 4:14)

All Christians have the duty to reproduce and find ways to nurse their spiritual children with the word of God.

Principle Of Quality: When talking about quality, we imply the qualities in the individual Christians i.e. what he is endowed with or what he can do. In other to quantify or assess the qualities in a person, some things would have to be looked into. They are: (1) His training (2) Talent (3) Education (4) Experience (5) Personality and (5) Wisdom. The combination of these forms the principle of quality. This can make one Christian more effective than the other.

Training: The training of a Christian matters in whatever he wants to accomplish in life. Everybody has certain training which can be described as the total sum of all his skills, including the ones he is not conscious of. So such skills form parts of potentials of Christians. For a Christian to boost his potentials, he must try as much as possible to acquire the skills that are relevant to his calling.

Talent: This is a natural ability to do a particular thing. Talent also plays a very important role in principle of qualities. Fortunately, Christians have the privilege to develop talents through the power of the Holy Spirit.

Education: Just as in the case of experience, education is in everyday activities of a person, what he has learnt in schools and influence of the people around him.

Experience: We all gather experience through various incidences, activities and the people we meet everyday. Experience in our daily activities is important because situations at times repeat themselves. That is the reason people say experience is the best teacher.

Personality: This has to do with the characteristics of a person. This may include his temperament, level of understanding and his attitude in general. Some people have strong personalities which placed them in leadership positions while some do not have the charisma of a leader. Christians, however, have the grace to develop the kind of personalities that can make them great leaders.

Wisdom: There is wisdom of God and wisdom of the world. The wisdom of the world is actually foolishness. The wisdom of God, according to Psalm 111:10, is actually the fear of God. If a person fears God, his ways will be that of God. He will carry out every word of God.

In so doing, he will see the way God sees things, do things in God's way and gets God's provisions and supernatural backings. So every Christian needs wisdom of God if he wants to realize his potentials. Without the wisdom of God, he will be doing things in the way of the world. The outcome may have eternal consequence.

Having gone this far with the course on Christian potentials, I pray that you begin to realize and maximize your potentials. I trust that you will begin to bear fruits now in Jesus name (Amen).

BUILDING YOUR SUCCESS AS A CHRISTIAN

AS A CHRISTIAN

(BOOK THREE)

INTRODUCTION

A friend of mine who is a civil engineer worked with me as a children teacher in a Church in Nigeria a few years ago on voluntary basis. This friend later traveled to London with high expectations. With his impressive qualifications and wealth of experience in civil engineering, he was expected to get a job without any problem. He was soon disillusioned when he could not find a job. Not willing to be an idle person, he went to a church, gathered the children and began to teach them the word of God; using stories as part of his tools to arrest their attentions. Before anyone knew it, his little children church had attracted all the young ones that normally roamed about the main church. Later, it was discovered that this friend of mine has the skill to handle children. He was employed instantly to work on Sundays as children teacher. If you think that is the end of the story, you are wrong. The children who learnt so much from my friend were fond of telling their parents about him. Most of them wanted them to invite him for dinner. Through that, he got to know a lot of people. Some of them later helped him to set up a small company all because he has positively influenced their children. He soon began to earn so much money - much more than what he expected from the job he tried to get.

In the above story, you can see that there is success in everything a man does, especially the ones that are done in the name of the Lord. In other words, there is success within each one of us. Preoccupation is what takes our minds away from the enormous opportunities available to us to make success even as a Christian. While many people see problems, very few see the solution to the problem as an opportunity to succeed. My friend did not know that the problem the children constituted in the Church was an opportunity to establish a children Church and also an engineering company. You can never know where the opportunity to solve a problem will take you to. John Lubbock said, *"What we see depends mainly on what we look for."* It follows, therefore, if all you can see in your environment is problem, it means all you are prepared to see is problem and all you will see is problem, not solution.

WHAT MAKES SUCCESS IN LIFE?

What makes success is the question everybody must ask himself. Is it money? Is it level of education? Is it connection? Is it fame? Is it marriage? To get the answer, we must define success.

What Makes A Success? Contrary to what many people think, success is not being wealthy or famous or in what you have achieved

41

but rather in living a purposeful and fulfilled life. It is not limited to one area of life. A man may be successful as a businessperson and still be a failure as a married man or even as a Christian. He may not be successful in acquiring wealth and yet a great success in other things like in the case of Florence Nightingale who came from a very rich family but sacrificed so much to serve humanity through nursing. Millionaire John Rockefeller admitted, *"I have made millions, but they have brought me no happiness."* The Bible says in Proverb 13:19, *"The desire accomplished is sweet to the soul...."* Success therefore depends on what you want to achieve with your life, how you go about it, the fulfillment of and in the achievement. As a Christian or a Church (the Body of Christ), success can imply visions and their implementations. These are important before anyone can feel fulfilled in life.

Following the above definition, we can broadly categorize what makes a success into two. They are goals that may be regarded as visions and their implementations. Before studying these two in building your success as a Christian, it is essential to note that the visions that are given by God to Christians are holy and precious seeds that meant to directly or indirectly bring about great harvest of souls to the kingdom of God. In other words, any vision which does not put eternity into consideration is either ambition of man or influenced by anti-Christ spirits.

Jesus said in Matthew 7:6, *"Give not that which is holy unto the dogs, neither cast ye your pearls before swine, lest they trample them under their feet, and turn again and rend you."* By implications of this passage, the Lord makes us to understand that no Christian can afford to give these holy seeds to unbelievers or cast them before people who the word of God considered as abominable. They would otherwise destroy the seeds and then turn against the person with the vision. I had lots of experience in this area. I once shared my visions with some people who claimed to be Christians but having wrong motives. God later warned me that I was casting my pearls before swine. Hence, I must get rid of the people I had involved in the visions. While doing that, I got into trouble. Before I knew it, I was neck deep with conflicts with carnal people who seemed ready to crush me and the vision. Since I was acting according to God's instruction, of course, I was able to overcome them.

GOALS

Zig Ziglar said in his book titled steps to the top, *"The poorest of all men is the one without a dream."* When you look at all the inventions we enjoy today, you will discover that they were once dreams of some people. A lot of people are miserable today because they do not have a dream that will make them lively. Such people may be wealthy or even famous yet they feel very dejected in life. One of the things that can bring life into a person is a dream - expectations. This is what I refer to as a goal in life. The goals you have set for yourself will engage your mind in certain activities which will make you lively and healthy mentally. Science proved that a lot of things depend on your brain, including the working condition of your body. Your mental alertness can help your body recover quickly if you fall sick. Similarly, the hopelessness of a person can bring about frustration and depression which can lead to mental sickness and death. It is therefore important that you set goals for yourself and be prepared to do something good with your life.

There are some characteristics in a good goal. They are: Measurable, Achievable, Communicable, Tangible and Definitive. Before we talk on each of them, you must understand that there are two types of goals. They are long term and short term goals. The long term goals are what will take years to accomplish such as building a career or a business empire or having branches of a ministries. The short term goals are the ones you have immediate plan to execute such as organizing a crusade or getting money for house rent or going for a short course. The major focus is on the long term goals that will determine what the future will look like and the way to get there.

Measurable: This aspect of a goal can be defined as a projection or calculation of what it takes to achieve the desired result. Consider what Jesus said in Luke 14:28-31 about building a tower (a laudable vision) without first thinking of the cost. This is where planning comes in although we shall still discuss that under implementation. When planning, you may or you may not foresee most of the obstacles or problems but definitely, if your goal is measurable, you can see what you want to achieve. John Foster Dulles said, *"the measure of success is not whether you have a tough problem to deal with, but whether it is the same problem you had last year."* The problem you face or foresee is not what makes your goal measurable or not but rather the ability to see from where you are the possibility of achieving the desired result in spite of the problem.

Achievable: When you want to set a goal, you must be realistic and be conscious of your limit. For instance, someone with physical impairment should not think of becoming a football star. Most things that people think cannot be achieved can be achieved. All it takes is faith, mental and physical work. The Bible defines faith in Hebrew 11:1 as the substance of things hope for, the evidence of things not seen. The most difficult and delicate part of any work is the mental work because so much depends on it. The ability to foresee or project the execution of a vision which seems unrealistic distinguishes a man with a vision from others. John Johnson said, *"Men and women are limited not by the place of their birth, not by colour of their skin, but by size of their hope."* If you believe you can build a castle in the air and you put what you have into it, you will end up building a mansion in a beautiful city. If your goal is to be achieved, you must have what it takes to achieve it. You need the faith, courage and determination - the attributes of mental work to achieve your goal. If you are afraid to face a cat, do not dare the lion. If David had dreaded the bear and the lion that threatened his father's sheep, he would not have had the courage or the vision to bring down Goliath. Sometimes people think they have set achievable goals but in fact they have not. Any achievable goal must be in proportion with what you are ready to offer or sacrifice.

Communicable: Most goals if not all need the support of other people before they can be achieved. It therefore follows that you must be able to carry people along with you in your goals. This is especially true with Church or team leaders or those who need the co-operations of other people. Since people are involved in most visions, there is need to communicate them to others before you can carry them along. John C. Maxwell in his book titled "The 21st Indispensable Qualities Of A Leader" gave four basic truths to follow to be effective communicator. They are: Simplify your message, Focus on the person whom you are communicating, Show the truth by believing in what you say and lastly seek response. In the book of Psalms chapter 78, the Word of God makes it necessary for a generation to communicate the law of God to another. So also a vision or goal must be communicable.

Tangible: Tangible in this regard means to be realistic, not imaginary. I have had to counsel a lot of youths who mentioned the people they loved to emulate. Many want to be football stars, while some would like to be music legends and others like that. This can be day-dream if they do not put what it takes to be so successful. What most youths do not understand is that people do not become successful by chance or through little efforts. Life is a matter of give and take what you can. Before you get anything from anything you must have given something in kind or cash. In most endeavours, you must give and give until you begin to get. A farmer who has his hands full of seeds must give some or all of the seeds before he can reap the harvest. If he puts nothing into the ground, he gets nothing. It is good to dream of greatness but there is a price to be paid. Clarence Munn says, *"the difference between great and good is a little extra effort."* For your vision to be tangible, it must be something you can work hard for. You cannot stand arm-folded and expect luck to do things for you. God loves to see His children making exploits. Those who do nothing and expect something will have nothing. The difference between tangible and unrealistic goals is the person that makes it real. Dr. J. A. Holmes said, *'never tell a young person that something cannot be done. God may have been waiting for centuries for somebody ignorant enough of the impossible to do that very thing.'* To illustrate this, I would relate the case of my brother-in-law called Tajudeen Dosumu. Taju went to a very primitive school in a village where he had his primary and secondary school education. His school certificate result in art subjects was very poor. He started working as a messenger in a Federal government establishment in Nigeria. When he was working, he had a goal to become a chemical engineer. That seemed unrealistic for someone who not only lack science background but also have a lot of obstacles to overcome. But he had one great advantage - a very strong desire to become a chemical engineer and faith in God. He worked very hard, communicating his goals to people including a deaf scientist who not only believed he could make it but also took time to teach him science subjects. He took another examination in science subjects and passed. Today, he holds a Masters degree and two BSc. degrees in both bio-chemistry (first class, University of Lagos in Nigeria) and chemical engineering (second class upper). He achieved his goal and rouse from the post of a messenger to the position of Standard Engineer Officer in the same establishment.

Definitive: This simply means specific and conclusive. Once a goal is set, there should be no going back. It takes determination to carry out goals because you will find every reason to change your mind. There are many things that prevent people from reaching their goals. Some of them include: (i) Fear of the unknown (ii) Indiscipline (iii) Indecision (iv) Fear of what people say or think and (v) Fear of failure.

When your goal is definitive, you need to begin to take steps and use the resources within your disposal to carry it out. The truth is: no one can use all the resources God had made available to him before he achieves a success. That is why the saying goes: 'when there is life, there is hope.' Zig Ziglar said, *'expect the best. Prepare for the worst.*

Take what comes.' If you do not take definitive step forward by doing all you can to achieve your goal, you will become stagnant water that offers nothing but stinks and dirty things. As stagnant water harbours and breeds all forms of disgusting objects that range from dead reptiles to fungus plants, so will the person that is not definitive in his goals harbour nothing good except excuses, complaint, criticism, animosity and even jealousy. Such person would learn to laugh at others when they are struggling to achieve their goals and becomes very jealous when they become successful. He will not only become an impediment to others but later a dependent on the success of others.

The above are the characteristics of reasonable goals or visions. We shall discuss implementation of goals as in relation to Successful Christianity.

IMPLEMENTATION OF GOALS

This is going to be our major focus. It is observed that most people have dreams or desires which I generally described as goals in life but they give up at the implementation stage. They settle for something far below their dreams and live in the dreams of other people who are strong enough to implement their own goals in life. Your goal in life is very important to you and to many others who would live after you. So you, the Body of Christ and the entire world cannot afford to let your dreams die for whatever reason. If you let it die, you have denied some people some things. Your children may be among them. I want you to see this world as a giant pot where people live and contribute their ideas that make life better for others. Such ideas may be in form of inventions, business, education, politics, research, medical field, entertainment, missionary work and so many other things. The ideas live on long after the owners have died. For instance, so many missionaries who came to Africa with the gospel did not only abolished so many barbaric customs but also established so many schools that made it possible to fight ignorance, which made it difficult for the continent to develop. Many of the schools exist till today. Do not think of coming into this world just to enjoy the ideas of others. Let others also enjoy your idea too. It is very important to make your life a success.

By now I assume you have a goal i.e. the thing you want to do with your time or your entire life. If you do not know what you want, let alone what you want to do, it is better you go over the previous discussion. You must have a goal first before you can think of implementation.

We are going to discuss a few things in this aspect of

46

implementation. These are: (i) Action plan (ii) Faith (iii) Preparation (iv) Opportunities.

ACTION PLAN

Someone said that failure to plan is a sure way to fail. Things do not happen by chance. To build a house, you need a plan. To establish any business, you need a plan called feasibility study report. To plant a church, you need a plan. To fight a battle with the enemy, you need a plan. Also to live any successful life, you need to plan for that life. You must plan the way you spend your time and money. Before you can implement your goal, you must plan. It is better to take years to plan what will take few weeks to achieve than to spend years trying anything without a plan. In the cause of planning, you may foresee some obstacles and find ways to overcome them. Note here that money is rarely the problem in implementations of goals or visions of a Christian and the Church but the attitude towards it. In Philippians 4:19, the Bible says, *'But my God shall supply all your needs according to his riches in glory by Jesus Christ.'* Remember the old sayings: *once there is a will, there is a way*. Big goals do not start big. They start very small with the little a person has. Nobody climbs the ladder from the top. You start from the first step. I know a woman who is now a big time business woman. She started it by selling few cups of salt. In most cases, businesses; endeavours and Church grow as persons with the vision grow in experience. When making action plan, be objective in your planning. Let your plan be in proportion with your desire to achieve your goal. To illustrate this, I would share with you the story of one of my classmates in secondary school. When we were in form one (Junior Secondary School one), this boy was the dullest student in class. When a student told another student, 'you are as dull as Victor,' (not real name) the student would get real mad. Victor did not get to the next class before he changed his plan from education to tailoring. He pursued the plan with passion. He became so successful that he was already using cars before any of us could graduate from the university. Education is very good, believe me, but if you do not have the strong desire that will see you all through, you better focus on something else. After all, if you can read and write, you can get informal education by reading on your own. One wonderful thing about reading is that you can become anything by reading. One of my course mates who lost his mother when he was a child became a college graduate without going to a secondary school. There was no magic about it. He simply had the desire to become a graduate and he

47

became one because he never gave up making personal efforts. When making action plan to implement your goals, you must put the followings into considerations:

(I) Is the goal short or long term?
(II) What does it take to implement the goal?
(III) What are my limitations and how do I overcome them?
(IV) What are the possible obstacles?
(V) Who and what do I need to reach my goals in spite of the obstacles?

If you can answer the above questions reasonably, you are already getting a blueprint of what you need to reach your goal. Note the word "reasonably." You do not need absolute answers to them before you can have a blueprint of your goal.

FAITH

Faith has to do with what and whom you believe in. Your faith matters a lot in whatever you do in life. Your faith will drive you to do so many things. You can describe faith as convictions or belief. Your faith must be in three things. They are: (i) Faith in God (ii) Faith in yourself (iii) Faith in your goals.

Faith In God: The Bible says in Hebrew 11:6, **'But without faith it is impossible to please him for he that cometh to God must believe that he is, and that he is the rewarder of them that diligently seek him.'** Faith in God makes a person conscious of the fact that He is everywhere. He is all powerful and all knowing.

Faith in God molds character, builds integrity and good relationship with others. Such faith makes a person to fear God. In the Book of Psalms 111:10, the Bible says, **'"The fear of the Lord is the beginning of wisdom: a good understanding have all they that do his commandments."** The fear of God not only makes a person wise but also godly. Your character and integrity matters in whatever you want to achieve in life. These are the ways to begin to build faith in God:

(I) It comes through reading and hearing the word of God everyday at home and in the church as the Bible says in Romans 10:17
(II) It is living by the word of God (Luke 4:4)
(III) Read books that will teach you more about God, not cult or other books that will lure you into violence or sins.
(IV) Move with godly people that will positively influence your life and avoid associating with ungodly people (Psalms 1:1-6). Make friends with people you can learn good things from, not with people that will influence you negatively.

48

Faith In Yourself: Ralph Waldo Emerson said, *"believe in yourself, and what others think won't matter."* Having faith in yourself does not mean you will not make mistakes but, irrespective of that, you need to believe in yourself that you can achieve what you want if you put all you can to get success. A lot of people fail because they lack confidence in themselves. They assume that they cannot achieve a thing without another person. They probably do not appreciate what the Bible says in Psalms 139:14 which states the fact that each person is fearfully and wonderfully made. In other words, each person in this world is a masterpiece of God. This can be proved from the fact that no one - dead or alive have the same fingerprints with another person. So there is no one of the type of anyone. Consequently, each has a gift and a mission peculiar to him. No one, therefore, must feel inferior or superior to another person, no matter highly gifted or intelligent or educated he may be. If you allow any trace of inferiority complex inside you, it is going to affect everything about you. One of the ways this is going to affect you is that the opinions of other people can make you surrender your vision to them. Because you feel inferior to them, you will feel their opinions are superior to yours. If you have a worthy vision, you must have confidence in it, even if it looks so simple or hard to achieve. I do tell people if they are more intelligent than me in what I desire to achieve, they cannot be more foolish. You may ask why taking pride in foolishness. My reason is found in 1 Corinthians 4:10 which says, *'We are fools for Christ's sake, but you are wise...'* So whatever a man is made up of, even if people consider it foolishness, it is to the glory of God as long as he is in Christ. I cannot help but to share with you the story of a man who displayed the above passage by writing it in front of his T shirt "I AM A FOOL" and added in much smaller letters, "for Christ's sake." People saw the big letters and started laughing at him. When he walked passed them, they discovered that he had a question for them at the back of the T shirt: "WHO'S FOOL ARE YOU?" That silenced those who were laughing at him. That indicates that no matter how wise a person may be, he is still a fool for something. So foolishness for the sake of Christ looks to me as a virtue all Christians we must covet. At least, we all know that God uses foolish things to confound the wise. Ordinarily, it was foolish of David to think of defeating Goliath who had been a warrior since he was young with a stone and a sling but God used that foolishness to give him victory. It was also foolish of Moses to think a way could be made for the people of Israel to pass on the sea with his rod but it worked out. What lies behind what looks like foolishness is the power

49

of God.

When you are conscious of the fact that you are masterpiece of God in His creation, you will have faith in yourself and your ability. You will not underrate yourself for any reason. Everybody is born with abilities. You must not feel inferior to the person with ten talents because you have only one. If you believe so much in that one and work so hard to use it, you can excel more than the person with ten. I was directing a Christian film at Ikenne-Remo in Nigeria where we could not get enough casts. Some of the ones we had were acting for the first time. Because it was a powerful production, my team was afraid to use weak Christians for the fear of spiritual attack. So we have to use the casts at our disposal. There was a fine sister who could have performed better than any of the new casts but for her feelings of inadequacy and lack of confidence in her ability. Having identified her problem, I told her to act herself if at all she could not pretend to be someone else. Fortunately, she was acting like someone preaching to a sinner. She eventually performed very well. Lack of confidence in yourself can affect your performance. So learn to build faith in yourself. Even if you are not yet good enough, keep telling yourself that you are going to do better. Do not listen to those who are looking for area of your weakness instead of strengths. Many critics, especially destructive type will never tell you that, with time and practice, you can improve on your skill even if they know you can. When you are attacked with criticism which you are going to face whether you like it or not, remember what Dale Carnegie said, *"any fool can criticize, condemn, and complain and most fools do."* You must understand that you know something which your critics do not know. So if there is anyone that will have more faith in you, it is you, yourself; not critics or friends or even family. Some people may have faith in you and what you can do with your potentials but if you do not have faith in yourself, it will amount to nothing. You must have faith that you have all it takes to carry out your goals in life, irrespective of what others think or say. Everybody has the potentials and the ability to excel in his chosen endeavour or career or ministries with time, practice and dedication. It is as simple as that. The followings are the ways you can start building faith in yourself.

(i) Engage yourself in the work that is relevant to your interest or gifts. Be involved in church activities, social or community works. If you cannot get someone to engage you, form a club that will engage and serve people for free. My friend never knew that God was preparing him for the work in the Church that would pay in London when he was teaching in Nigeria on voluntary basis. As you engage yourself in what seems minor, you will be building the skill and faith in yourself.

(ii) Spend quality time to study and share what you have learned with other people. This can help you overcome certain weakness which you may not be aware of. Apart from that, you will begin to gain confidence in your communication skill which is vital if you really want to communicate or share your vision with others.

(iii) Identify the area of your weakness that poses threats to your goal and discipline yourself to overcome it. If you eat too much, put yourself into fasting. If you are extravagant, cut down your expenses. If you sleep too much, cultivate the habit of walking round the room while you read. If you are always afraid, always face the thing you fear so much. As you grow over your weakness, you will begin to build more confidence in yourself. Gilbert Arland said, *"when an archer misses the mark he turns and looks for fault within himself. Failure to hit the bull's-eye is never the fault of the target. To improve your aim, improve yourself."*

(iv) Always take up the challenges people always shy away from, especially in the Church even if you know the price is great. That is what would make you outstanding and full of faith. Consider the common characteristics in the people that strive for excellence in the second book of Timothy 2:3-6. The people are a soldier in verse 4, an athlete in verse 5 and a farmer in verse 6. The three of them have these in common. They are always full of (a) discipline (b) endurance (c) determination (d) readiness to face challenges and (e) hope to get desired result. These must be present in anyone who desires any success in life. After all, life is a challenge. So take up the challenge which others shy away from.

Faith In Your Vision Or Goal: To have faith in any goal, you must have a goal which must have the characteristics which had been explained earlier. It is not enough to have a goal that is measurable, achievable, communicable, tangible and definitive. You must have faith in the goal. John C. Maxwell said, *"a difficult crisis can be more readily endured if we retain the conviction that our existence holds a purpose, a cause to pursue, a person to love, a goal to achieve."* There are some factors that determine the growth of faith in your goal. But first, it is instructive to note that the faith you have in your goal will determine how far you can go in the midst of oppositions. Every good goal always faces oppositions, some of which are fierce enough to make you give it up. The good news is: you can achieve what you want to achieve. Theodore Epp says, *"our strength is seen in the things we stand for; our weakness is seen in the things we fall for."* If you fall for the opposition to give up your goal, you are weak and you are not worthy of that goal. The Bible says in Proverbs 24:10, *'If you faint in the day of adversity, your strength is small.'* If you really have a goal in life, your faith in it will sustain you in the days you are forced to give it up. It may be mere criticism that will try to lay you off your plan. David Brinkley said, *"a successful man is one who can lay a firm foundation with bricks others have thrown at him."* The bad news about giving up your goal is that you will find it more difficult to achieve another good goal, no matter how promising it may be. But if you press on in your goal, you will find enough strength to continue as you hang on. When you succeed in carrying out your goal, you will have more strength and confidence to go for greater goal like Alexander, the great who got more and more powerful as he conquered one empire after the other until there was no more empire for him to conquer. If you do not have faith in your goal, do not attempt to achieve it because it will be tried. John C Maxwell said, *'if your vision doesn't cost you anything, it is daydream.'* Only your faith in it will make it stand. Henry James makes us to understand that until we try, we don't know what we can't do. Zig Ziglar encouraged, *'keep trying. It is only from the valley that the mountain seems high.'* In other words, the height of your goal does not matter. It is the height of your faith in it that matters. You may set a small goal and still fail if you don't have enough faith in it to make it succeed. The factors responsible for growth of faith in a goal are as follows:

(I) The more information and the more you know about your vision, the more your faith in it. If you learn about your vision, the more your convictions that it can be achieved.

(ii) The people you associate with are another good factor that can make your faith to grow or die. Do you associate with people who have no goals for their lives? Mark Twain said, *"Keep away from people who belittle your ambition. Small people always do that but the really great people make you feel that you, too, can become great."* If you are always in the company of those who will encourage you, your faith in your goal in life will increase. Share your goals in life only with those who will encourage you, not those who will discourage you or kill your goal with pessimism. The Bible says in Philippians 3: 2, **'Beware of dogs, beware of evil workers, beware of the concision.'**

(iii) The time you spend, planning and thinking of your goal in life will help your faith in it to grow. When you spend more time, planning and thinking about your goals, you will foresee hindrances and ways to overcome it. You must note that there is nothing like hassle free vision. Everything a man wants to achieve in life has some elements of difficulties and even risks built inside it.

(iv) Take some steps towards your goal, no matter how minor it may be. The steps you have taken so far to achieve your goal will increase your faith in it. If you can, create an environment that will make it very difficult for you to give up. For instance, when I was working as a civil servant in Nigeria, I had the vision to become a writer, publisher, teacher and film producer that would evangelize all categories of people including children. It was a good job because I was well paid but it was a serious hindrance for me to carry out my vision. I had a lot of people depending on my salary but I knew I had to resign my appointment with the government if I must carry out vision. Considering the economic problem in the country, it would be foolish, if not crazy to resign. I became very unpopular in my family when I left the job because I no longer had any source of income. I have to struggle hard to carry out my vision and prove I knew what I was doing. It took me time but I began to reach my goal. I published my first book which is not really a book. It was so appreciated that I sold several thousands of copies in 2002. The profit was so much that I used it to establish a primary school for my wife. Today, I have had the grace to publish many books locally and internationally and the privilege to produce a number of films for evangelism and edification of Body of Christ. Vince Lombardi said, 'the harder you work, the harder it is to surrender.' You must work out your success yourself. Nobody is going to work it out for you. The Bible says in Proverbs 20:4, 'The sluggard will not plow by reason of the cold; therefore shall he beg in the harvest, and have nothing.'

PREPARATION

Contrary to general opinion, preparation to achieve a goal is in everyday activities. It is not only in what you are taught in the school or what you read in books or in the people you meet everyday but also in what you do everyday. What you do today is your preparation for tomorrow. If you invest your time playing piano, the chances are that you may become a professional pianist. Whatever you spend your time doing is what you will improve upon. There were times in my life when all I was doing was to read and write. You can judge if there is trace professionalism in my writings. If you spend your time partying, you will end up a destitute that depends on others for survival. Zig Ziglar said, *"the present day is important to you for this reason: you can waste it or use it, but no matter how you spend it, you've traded a day of your life for it."* Joseph C. Grew has this to say, *"we cannot pause, or hesitate, or kill time as if you could kill time without injuring eternity."* The Bible makes us to understand in Ecclesiastes 3:1-8 that there is a season and a time for everything, including a time to be born and to die. You have the options of spending your time preparing to reach your goal or to spend it watching meaningless television programs or films instead of reading, spend so much time chatting on the internet instead of gathering information that will help you reach your goal or spend the whole day with friends who have not focus. In anything anyone wants to achieve in life, there is no shortcut. Shortcuts shorten success and sometimes life. A man who steals or robs others only risk going to jail or getting killed. A man who is dishonest only risks losing his job and his integrity with others, thereby finding it difficult to get an employment or risks not having people doing business with him. A student who cheats during the examination only risks being caught. There is no shortcut to success in life.

When preparing to reach your goal, you must work on the followings: (i) Your attitude (ii) Your skill and (iii) Resources. We shall treat each as they relate to preparation. Before then, it is instructive to note that preparation is the first thing you need to make before you can make best use of the opportunity to reach your goal. As Myles Munroe said, success comes when preparation meets with opportunities. Of the two, you can only control one which is preparation.

Your Attitude: Your attitude is your greatest asset or major obstacle to achieve your goal in life. Attitude is the starting point of any success in life - be it in marriage, ministries, and business or in anything. Your attitude has a lot to do with the way you think, how you feel or react to any situation. It also has to do with what you say and do. If what you say match what you do, you will build the integrity that will help you reach your goal. If they do not match, you will be seen as inconsistent or even dishonest. In business, honesty is regarded as the best policy anywhere. As for Christians, the attributes that are stated in 2 Peter 1:5-8 are very essentials to be successful and prosperous. These attributes includes diligence, faith, virtues (which can be attributed to fruits of the Spirit that are stated in Galatians 5: 22-23), knowledge, temperance, patience, godliness, brotherly kindness and charity. Christians have all the chances to excel in their chosen

54

careers but many seem far away from success. Some Christian business, organizations and even ministries are not achieving their objectives. Some are trying in vain the methods that are common among non-Christians. One needs to ask why since God promises His people a lot of blessings in the book of Deuteronomy 28:1-13. There is need for Christians or the Church to retrace their steps. Where have things gone wrong? Is it God that has changed His mind about the promises or the problem is with the Christians. We know for sure that God can never change His mind. The Bible says in Ezekiel 24:14, *'I the Lord have spoken it: it shall come to pass. I will not go back, neither will I spare, neither will I repent; according to thy ways, and according to thy doings, shall they judge thee, says the Lord God.'* From this passage, we can see that God also blesses his people according to their ways (attitudes), not just because He has promised them. To be successful therefore in anything at all, the following Biblical principles must followed:

(i) You need to seek the kingdom of God first as in Luke 12:31
(ii) You must follow the Word of God. That is the condition attached to the blessings in Deuteronomy 28: 1-13.
(iii) You need to pay your tithes and offerings in the house of God which is the command in Malachi 3:8-12 if you really want to involve God in your work or business.
(iv) You need to allow others to benefit from your blessings according to Luke 12:33.
(v) Your worship and service in the house of God cannot be compromised, no matter how busy you are in your place of work. Since Christians are members of Body of Christ, they must play their roles as in 2 Corinthians chapter 12.

For you to prepare to achieve your goal, you must do all you can to improve on your attitude. Everybody needs positive attitude towards everything in life, towards his enemies and in stormy situations. Kenneth Copeland said, *'your gift will take you places but your character will keep you there.'* Since people are the reflection of what a person is in the inside, he will seem surrounded by nice people if he is nice to them. Anyone with problem of attitude will seem surrounded by mean people. I know a man who despite the fact that he was not rich made people happy. He loved to visit people in their homes to know how to pray and meet their needs. Somehow through prayers and personal commitment, he always found solutions to their problems. This man fell sick one day. He was in dire need of blood before he could survive. News about his condition spread round the town. Guess what. The whole town stormed the hospital, ready to drain their blood for that man. If there is anything we must improve in our lives it is our attitudes. Christians through selfless service and holy living are to be role models. Through that alone they can be successful in many areas of their lives. The problem most Christians face is in the area of self will and indecisions to sacrifice their personal conveniences for others. Few people appreciate the fact that some people would not be blessed if others do not make sacrifices and yet all ask blessings from God. This brings to my mind how a teenager won an entire family for Christ during the inhumane military regime in Nigeria.

The family was starving. A teenager went to the family to preach the word of God to them. The father who could not think of anything but how to feed his children and their mother had threatened to deal ruthlessly with the preacher boy. "If you don't get out of this house," the man bellowed at him, "you will be sorry." The boy did not give up. He left the house and came back with some food for the family. That gesture of love won the entire family for Christ. That kind of attitude is needed to build success in life. Do all you can to improve on your attitude through selfless services and support of others instead of thinking of yourself alone. Edward Bulwer Lytton said, *"a good heart is better than all the heads in the world."* I remember a teacher who mercilessly beat a boy in his class to extent that he sustained a permanent bump on the fore head for a trivial offence. Even though the teacher was unrepentant but because the parents are Christians, they not only forgave him but also taught the boy to forgive him. Years later, the boy became a lecturer in a university at the time the teacher was just going for a degree course in the same institution. The lecturer recognized him and went to identify himself to the teacher. The teacher began to apologize for his negative attitude many years before. We all have a chance to show a little kindness to our follow human beings. You can never tell what it means to your success in life or what it will fetch you in future. I cannot help but to share with you the story of a man who struggled to take care of the twin brothers in Nigeria. The brothers later traveled to America. After some years, they came for a visit in Nigeria and decided to see the man that took care of them. They found him in the same condition they had left him. These twin brothers helped the man to get to America where he became a successful person. You have probably heard that both good and evil have their rewards. The one you are involved in will determine where you will end up. Robespierre said, *"no man can climb out beyond the limitations of his own character."*

Your Skill: This is what makes you a valuable asset to yourself, your family, the Church and the world. What you know add value to you. For instance this book you are reading is not worth spending your time reading if it is blank paper. But value had been added to it by the teachings. The teachings may not worth studying if they have nothing to offer you. The same thing is applicable to an individual. The greatest asset in a country is the number of active and skillful people the nation has, not the amount of wealth it has. People who do not contribute their manpower resources into the economy eat out the reserve of the nation. So no matter how rich a country may be in natural resources, if there are no good hands to manage and add value to what is on ground, the people will soon become poor in the midst of plenty. That is why many countries, especially in Africa are still poor in the midst of plenty. Those who are supposed to be acquiring skills in schools or other places are already nursing babies that would later depend on others for survival. The number of beggars and touts in the streets in some rich countries like Nigeria is staggering. So many children who are supposed to be in schools are asking for alms everyday. Many people in these countries depend so much on the government to give them everything they need. Government should not only get them employment but also provide the food and cook it for them. People who expect so much from their governments without making efforts to help themselves become frustrated. When they get frustrated, they turn to robbery or prostitution or other anti-social activities. What baffles me most in people is the amount of skills that are not used. Plutarch said, *'the richest soil, uncultivated produces the rankest weeds.'* Many nations like Nigeria are rich in everything - natural and human resources but the country is full of thick weeds like political, economic problems and social vices because of lack of skillful and cultured people.

Since there is no free lunch anywhere in the world and since life is give and take, each person must give in kind, goods or service before he or she can get something in return. Even God will never bless idle hand. When God created Adam and Eve, he told them to till the ground. J. G. Holland said, *'God gives every bird its food, but He does not throw it into the nest.'* You can see why you have to add value to yourself by acquiring skills before you make success in your endeavours. You need to work towards your goals or vision by developing the skill you need.

These are the ways to develop your skill:
(a) You must constantly practice what you want to develop within you.

57

Macauley said, *"just remember that if you are not working at your game to the utmost of your ability, there will be someone out there somewhere with equal ability. And one day, you'll play each other, and he'll have the advantage."*

(b) You must learn from other people who are skillful in the area. You also learn from your mistakes and of others.

(c) Ask questions, no matter how foolish they sound. An inquisitive mind always enriches the head with knowledge. If you do not understand what you are being taught in the school, do not be too shy or proud to ask questions. If you do not ask questions about what you don't know, you will miss the opportunity to add more to your knowledge. After all, no one can claim to be an island of knowledge. I remember asking my biology class teacher when he was teaching us about insects in junior secondary school. I said almost foolishly, "sir, can you explain why God created flies, since it has nothing good to offer to mankind except diseases?" That question sounded so funny that everybody including the teacher laughed. The teacher made me realized that it was an intelligent question because he could see that I wanted to know about life circle which was meant for the higher class. He repeated the question in other classes and among the teachers. I became a star in that school for asking question that almost sounded so foolish. I also asked lots of questions from the person that taught me some film techniques.

(d) You must cultivate the habit of reading books related to your career, not just any book. Through that you can learn from others. I read some of the books that are used to train teachers by National Teachers' institute, Kaduna in Nigeria because I want to develop the skill in teaching young ones and in writing for them. They are lots of books. It was like I was going on course without an instructor but the knowledge I acquired from the books justify my efforts to study them. Although I do not possess the certificate of a teacher but I can teach just like any good teacher and also write like any other good children book writer. In fact, the book titled 'The Young Generation Story book' is used by some professional Christian teachers to teach children in primary schools and Churches. I did not get the skills by chance. Nothing like skills comes by chance. Even if a person is gifted, he would still need to develop that gift. I learned from professionals through their books. Skills are all there for everyone to acquire. You have to discipline yourself enough to acquire them. Skills make the difference between professionals and amateurs or unskilled labourers just as ability to work distinguishes a worker from a destitute who has no service to offer.

(e) You must have the passion to acquire the skill. This will cause you to explore every chance to develop the skill you need to reach your goal. John C Maxwell said, *"if you follow your passion - instead of other's perceptions - you can't help becoming a more dedicated, productive person."*

RESOURCES

Resources can be divided into three broad categories. They are (1) Money (2) Materials and (3) Manpower. We are going to discuss each as they are related to this course.

Money: Money had always been a source of great controversy all over the world from time immemorial. The Bible says in 1 Timothy 6: 10, 'For the love of money is the root of all evil: which while some coveted after, they have erred from faith, and pierced themselves with many sorrows.' Money can be a good source of evil, problem and sorrow according to that passage and yet we all need money. Every organization, ministry, business or individual needs money to operate successfully. Without money one can hardly achieve anything. Money is used in business, it is used to pay salaries of workers, it is used to pay school fees, it is used to maintain ourselves and to do all sorts of things that relate to life and everyday activities. The question now is: How can a Christian make God's kind of money? The following principles are the general ways.

(a) First of all, you need a vision or a marketable idea from God. This vision will involve meeting people's need since you are going to make money through them. A lot of people think they need money first before they can execute a project. It is not necessarily so. What a person needs for a start is the idea or knowledge of what he wants to do. As pointed out earlier, there is no free lunch anywhere. You cannot touch people's pockets without meeting their needs or touching their hearts unless you want to steal from them. You probably paid for this book before you got it. If it does not suit what you want, you may not buy it. Similarly, if you do not market things or render any service, you would probably be begging for alms.

(b) After getting a vision or a marketable idea, you need to learn or get information about what you want to do. In most cases, you need to connect with people who will help you one way or the other. There are so many people who are looking for where to invest their money. Most of them may not be interested in your idea but there is someone God has ordained to help you if the idea is actually from Him. You need to wait and pray for the person to show up.

A man came to tell me that he had discovered a non-alcoholic beer and asked me how he could make a success out of it. I asked him what makes his discovery a beer if it is non-alcohol. He shared the details with me which I have to accept because it was not my field. I thought of introducing him to an expert in the field but I know he would ask me if the chemical contents in what he called non-alcoholic beer had been analyzed. I told him to make efforts to find a laboratory where it can be analyzed but I never see him again. He probably expected me to tell him how to get the money to finance the project. He did not know I was ready to offer him what he really needed - link him with the experts that will help him achieve his goal to make a non-alcoholic beer.

(c)   If you have the money to spend on your idea, why not spend it? If do not spend, the idea will die a natural death. You have probably heard the adage that says: nothing ventured, nothing gained. The risk a man refused to take will affect him in his progress. A progressive person is always prepared to take calculated financial risk.

When I was going into publishing business, I have to save some money that was very hard to get at that time. I published the first edition of Calvary Rock Periodical in 1995 in Nigeria, hoping to get more money when it was launched. It was a flop. I had to save some money the following year before I could afford to publish another edition. Again, it was a flop. The printer's devil came with his ugly performance and messed up the whole publication. In the process of all these, I was learning vital lessons; knowing fully well that the income of each year of my life is going into the publication. I waited again for another year to gather some money and put it into the publication. At last, I got the result I wanted. In fact, that edition launched me into film production. If you believe in your idea, you will spend what you have on it and if you want to make money, you must spend money.

(d)   You need to be meticulous and very prudent in the way you spend your money. A good business man knows that if he wants to have more money, he must increase his income and cut down his expenses wherever possible. For this reason, companies are aggressive in marketing their products or services. Every amount of money a person wastes will affect him. No one can afford to waste money.

Material: Contrary to what most people think, material is not limited to physical things like crude oil and other things that can be used for production, materials can also come in form of ideas. Such materials (in the form of ideas) can be changed into finished product (in the form of services). The most neglected material in the whole world today is ideas. All goods and services you see around are products of ideas. A friend of mine who is a motivational speaker, Mobolaji Sodiya said, *"the most important commodity in the world of business is a marketable idea that is properly implemented and extensively publicized."*

You need to come up with ideas. When you have one, you are naturally getting ready to reach your goal. The world is full of material resources which includes the ideas inside you and me. Many people including the ones with ideas are becoming liabilities to their countries instead of becoming lots of blessings. If everybody is contributing his ideas to the numerous materials on ground, a lot of problem in the country will disappear. No matter how blessed the world is with physical materials, it would amount to nothing if there are no people with ideas to bring them into use. For instance, the building you reside in would be nothing but sand if there is no idea to assemble the materials together to make it a building. In short, ideas make useless things valuable. Everything a person needs to excel in life is within him and everything a country needs to be prosperous is within the country. There are many countries that are not as blessed as others in terms of natural and human resources but because the people have ideas, they are far more prosperous than the countries that are blessed with natural resources. Why? The solution can be explained under manpower resources.

Manpower: It is not possible to treat everything about manpower resources even in a single course. It is too complex for that. However, we shall treat the very primary aspect of it as it relates to building your success as a Christian. Manpower resources have to do with human beings. To begin with, I want to paint the picture of the potentials of human beings in relation to money and material resources through the story of a woman and her children.

It was during the stiff regime of the military in Nigeria, the time things were very tough for everyone, that this woman lost her husband; leaving her with three children to cater for. This woman has two options that were common for survival. She either resolved to steal or go into prostitution. The other alternative was to get a job. This was nearly impossible because many businesses were folding up.

Most of the existing ones owned their workers several months' salaries. That was the situation the woman found herself. As a Christian, she knew she must not sell herself to the rich men that were ready to take advantage of her condition even though there were three children that were counting on her to survive. The woman made up her mind that she would rather die than to sin against God. Because of that firm decision, she found the way out of the problem. She went to those selling bean cakes known in the country as "akara". To make the bean cakes, the coats of all the beans would have to be removed and washed away with water before it is grinded and fried with oil. Most of the people who sell this type of food do not know that the coats of the beans are very nutritious. So they always throw them away. This woman explained her condition to those selling bean cakes in other to get their co-operation. She would tell them that all she needed as help was for them to reserve for her the coats of the beans instead of throwing them away. She would get the bean coats at times with some beans which the people would deliberately leave for her. She would grind, pack it in tins and cook it in a pot. She not only provided food for herself and her children but also sold some to get money to buy other things they need in the house. As long as there were people that were selling the bean cakes, she would get food to eat. Today, her story has changed. She now lived a more comfortable life with her children. People say necessity (or even poverty) is the mother of invention. I quite agree because a man may not make full use of his head if he gets all the comfort he needs. That is why people must see every problem as an opportunity to make best use of their potentials, not excuses to be involved in malpractice. This can be done by simply studying the problem and finding ways to solve the one you feel you can solve. The problems of diseases which are expensive to cure in Nigeria for instance is causing the business of orthodox medicine to boom, making many people to become millionaires within few years.

Most things depend on manpower resources. It is man that combines resources together and brings good result. If manpower is very defective, other resources would be wasted or made useless. If other resources are defective, manpower resource can make them effective. Man creates things with his creative ability by maneuver or add value to the materials which had been provided in abundance by God. God did not create anything again after creating the world and human beings. He had created everything for the world to advance right from the beginning. In other words, everything you see around comes from the earth which God created. It is man that reproduce everything we enjoy today with the natural resources. Cars, houses, money, computers - name it - were all made from the ground except, of course, if someone wants to point out the ones that drop from the sky. Nothing is ever a product of accident as some people think. It takes the creative power of someone to bring them into being. God created man in His image and man with the creative power he inherit from his Maker recreated or reproduces all the things we see around. I expect that to make sense to everybody. Anyone who thinks he can reach his goal in life by accident is only waiting to reach his grave probably by accident.

Everybody on earth has a mission assigned to him by God but there is no way he can know or understand the assignment without knowing God through His Son, Jesus Christ. Although many are able to perceive their missions through their natural gifts but they cannot excel in it as they ought to without knowing God. If someone does not know or understand the purpose of his being, two things can happen. He will either use his talent to create limited success for himself with the creative power God has given to people or he will be used by the devil. If he creates success through his natural gift, putting God aside, he is not likely going to feel fulfilled in life. That is why many rich people die with sorrow. While some people commit suicide like one of the richest man in the world who took his own life, others who successfully use what they have according to God's plan for their lives die with joy and fulfilment.

I remember the story of a two boys who used to go to the church together. As they grow up, one became interested in making money while the other wanted to know more about God. The boy who wanted to become rich went to the city and became fabulously rich many years later. The other boy settled down with his family and God. One day, the rich man remembered his old friend and sent for him. His friend could not even afford the cost of transportation to the city. So he sent him some money to cover all his traveling expenses. The rich man and his friend later had a chance to reflect the old days after he had shown him much of his wealth. His friend said, 'you've shown me so much of what you have down here. What about the one up there?' He pointed to the sky to let him know that he referred to heaven. The rich man confessed, 'I don't think I have anything up there. In fact, I wish I can have your type of peace.'

A lot of people look for money at the expense of their salvation while some are focused on doing the will of God. When a man is doing the will of God, using what he has at his disposal, he will not only please God but also please himself, feeling peaceful; joyous and

63

fulfilled. The followings are what make manpower very defective or dangerous or a failure:

(A) _Greed Or Selfishness._ The Bible says in Proverbs 3:27-28, **'withhold not good from them whom it is due, when it is in the power of your hand to do it. Say not unto your neighbour, Go, and come again, and tomorrow I will give; when you have it with you.'** Greed or selfishness is lack of consideration for others. When a person is concerned about himself alone, he will be surrounded by unfriendly people who are equally interested in themselves alone. Christians must not be interested in themselves alone if they want to be successful. One of the characteristics a Christian must exhibit is selflessness and generosity. Richard Foster advised, _"just the very act of letting go of money, or some treasures, does something within us. It destroys the demon of greed."_ John Bunyan has this to say, _"you have not lived today until you have done something for someone who can never repay you."_

(B) _Pride:_ This cannot only make a person a failure but can also destroy everything good, according to Proverb 16:18 and 29:23. No one has any reason to be proud because we are all picked from the dust. Sooner or later our bodies will go back to the dust. We did not bring anything into this world and we shall take nothing. A good looking person did not create himself and no one can say a woman is too beautiful to be thrown into grave when she dies. Likewise, a wise person cannot claim he gets his wisdom through his efforts. So there is no basis for pride in life. Not only does God resents pride, people also dislike proud people. If you want to deal with people, you must be humble. Ministers too must be humble in the way they present Christ to others. There must not be any trace of holier-than-thou attitude in anything they do even if they know they are not on the same level with sinners. People in business appreciate that they need to be humble and tolerant in the way they deal with their customers if they want to remain in business.

(C) _Laziness:_ This can make man a complete failure. The Bible says in Proverbs 6:9-11, **'How long will you sleep, O sluggard? When will you arise out of your sleep? Yet a little sleep, a little slumber, a little folding of the hands to sleep: So shall your poverty come upon you like a vagabond, and your want like an armed man.'** A person who cannot work with his hands or brain will end up a destitute. When waiting for God to make way for him in his business or career, a Christian must be doing something that will earn him his income or enhance his skill or value in life. Conrad Hilton said,

"Success seems connected with action. Successful people keep moving. They make mistakes, but they don't quit."

(D) Ignorance: This is another factor that can make a person a failure. The Bible says in Hosea 4:6 that the people of God are destroyed for lack of knowledge. Note the difference between knowledge and wisdom. Knowledge is what a person knows - the information he has. Wisdom is synonymous to intelligence. So it is possible to be wise and not knowledgeable. When a person lacks information about a particular thing, he is said to be ignorant of that thing. People go to school, not because they are foolish but because they do not want to be ignorant. When a person is born, he has nothing in his head but brain that can be compared with blank tape. As he grows, he begins to gather information which he will later interpret as he grows up. At the age he is able to comprehend the information, he begins to learn some things. What he learns or develops within himself in his environment would make him either valuable to the people and the country or useless or even at times dangerous to the nation. If he learns the right thing, he would be a blessing to the country but if he learns the wrong thing, he would pose a very serious problem or a threat to many things including lives.

In every given society, community, organization or group; human capital are the most valuable assets. For anyone to prepare himself to become a valuable asset, he must do the followings:

(i) Make proper evaluation of yourself by identifying your talents, gifts, interest, abilities and disabilities. Through that, you can know what you can achieve with your life. You may have ten talents and think you have five. You may have the ability to teach and think all you can do is to read. Think of the good things people are saying about your gift. Do not mind cynics who think you cannot achieve a thing. When I was in school, I was so poor in science subjects that I dared not think of becoming a scientist. So I worked hard on art subjects, especially English language and literature since I planned to become a writer. I write stories and essays and gave them to my friends to read. Their responses really encouraged me. In fact some used to argue that I must have gone to copy them somewhere. When you identify your abilities and disabilities, you must begin to work on them by putting them into practice and making up for them respectfully.

(ii) Make up your mind never to compromise your Christian faith even if others compromise. Take stand against all forms of sins or evils. You will be taking stand with God if you do. I like to quote Edmund

Burke all the time. He said, *"the only thing necessary for the triumph of evil is for good men to do nothing."* Let people know what you stand for. If they know this, they wont persuade you to commit sin. The Bible says in 1 Thessalonians 5:22, **'Abstain from all appearance of evil.'**

(iii) After you have made up your mind to take stand with God by living a holy life, you must add value to yourself by acquiring knowledge and skill. You do not need to do a job because of the money you will get from it alone but also to acquire skill. You will need the skill long after you have spent all the money you make from it. Sometimes, it is good to work for free if it will enhance your value or skill. The case of my civil engineer friend in London is a classic example. If you graduate in the school, instead of waiting for nothing to happen, take up a teaching job even if they are paying you nothing to write home about. Who knows if that will give you the breakthrough you need like my engineer friend. Unknown to many people, the service they render in the house of God always add to their values or skills. I know of so many successful gospel musicians who began their careers as Church choirs. My talent in acting was developed when I was a children pastor. The children always forced me to interpret many roles with action whenever I was telling them stories. They wanted to know how a fish swims. They wanted to hear the dog barking. I remember how I fell down from the table while trying to show the children how a monkey jumped from one tree to another. They laughed at me and asked if that was the way monkey fell from the tree. I replied, 'no! I'm not a monkey. That's why I fell. It's hard for a monkey to fall from the tree.'

OPPORTUNITIES

You have probably heard that opportunity comes once in a while. That may not be true to some extent. The opportunity to excel is always around. The reason most people don't see it is because it is sometimes buried somewhere. It is sometimes flying. You have to search for it as if you are looking for hidden treasures. You ca also catch an opportunity as if you are trying to catch a bird. The good news is: it is always around. You will find it if you make efforts to look for it. The bad news is: it will always fly away if you are not prepared to catch it. No matter how much you try, you cannot catch the opportunity if you are not prepared. That is why I have taken time to take you through the period of preparation. With the advent of modern technology, opportunities are flying like birds all over the world. You can catch some through the newspapers, the internet, radio, television, in the school, in the street - everywhere. But the problem is many people are not prepared for the opportunities that are flying around. John C Maxwell advised, *"don't wait for opportunity to knock. Opportunity doesn't come to the door knocking. You've got to go out and look for it. Take stock of your assets, talents, and resources. Doing that will give you an idea of your potentials... opportunity is everywhere."* The length of preparation and the amount of value you have added to yourself will determine how you will soar.

Some people are like chicken that see every creeping thing as opportunity to eat, spending the whole day picking the ground. People in this category are common. They do not see beyond their immediate environment. So they see little things like employment or going abroad as golden opportunities to be comfortable. Instead of ploughing for harvest, they pick the ground and settle for something relatively small. If someone in the class of uncommon bird comes with an idea that works, the people in the class of chicken flock to do the same thing as if there is no other idea that works. They cannot try new ideas, break new ground and try to invent because they are thinking of immediate income. Zig Ziglar said, *"go as far as you can see, and when you get there you will always be able to see further."*

Another class of people we have can be compared with a hawk. These people only see the opportunities to use others to their own advantages. They are not interested in exploring opportunities to excel even though they can see it. They do not have many ideas but they know how to steal other people's ideas. They have good eyes to see far and beyond because of their position in life but they would never use it for the good of others. Instead, they take undue advantage of a lot of chicken, especially the young ones who have no experience of how to protect themselves or their potentials. They use these young ones as political thugs, assassins and armed robbers. Some made prostitutes out of the girls that are young enough to be their grand children while some lure young girls from their parents and use them as sex workers in other countries. Others sometimes use inexperienced people to push hard drugs and made them to face jail sentence in the country that is far from their homes. I can never exhaust all the atrocities of these hawks but I want to relate the case of a girl who sold her future for temporary pleasure. Her story was published in a newspaper some years ago. She had boyfriends, including sugar daddies that meet her needs when she was in school. One day, one of her boyfriends took her to a house where there were three other men. She was entertained with some drink that was mixed with some drug. She was not herself after taking the drinks, acting like a wild girl as the three men slept with her. After coming back to her senses, she knew she must not mess around with just any man. She later fell in deep love with a man that was ready to make life very comfortable for her. Soon they began to plan for their wedding but somehow, the man's brother in US stumbled on a pornographic magazine and saw this girl sleeping with three men. The page of the magazine was sent to the man who later sent it to her family. Of course, that put an end to the marriage proposal. These men are hawks, the type of people that sell the future of young people for their selfish interest. It is up to you to redeem your future by saying firm "NO" to anything sinful, no matter the temporary relief or pleasure it will earn you. The Bible says in Proverbs 11:3, *'the integrity of the upright shall guide them: but the perverseness of the transgressors shall destroy them.'* In the ocean of insanity, if you keep your sanity in Christ, you will survive. The girl allowed the hawks to get her but she was lucky that she did not catch HIV. So she can still gather her life together again. You must not look for a cheap way out. You must see yourself as being all alone with God on your side in the struggle. If help comes from someone on time - fine. If not, like Winston Churchill said to some college students, *"never, never, never give up."*

The other class of people we have are those that can be compared with eagles and eaglets, the uncommon birds. These people do not see the way others see because they are visionary. They operate from the level that is not common to either the chicken or the hawk. They know what they want and how to get it. They do not see any difficulty in achieving their goals as long as it is possible because they know they can be what they want to be if they put enough efforts into it. As the eagles soar in the air, seeing all opportunities to get what they want either in the water or on the land or on top of the trees, these people can imagine what they want and can see how to get it right on their beds. As strong as lions are, they cannot see as much opportunities as the eagles. Likewise, people that are compared with eagles may not be as powerful or wealthy or well connected like people that can be compared with lions but they see opportunities to excel more than others. They are always preparing themselves to fly higher than other birds because that is what makes them outstanding. The eagles do not go after what the chickens or hawks go after. They are different from those that step over one another to get chicken feeds. Eagles cannot be caged like other birds. They would die trying to get out. The good news about all these classes of people is that anybody can choose to be what he wants to be. It is not a matter of luck or destiny but a matter of choice.

I see people struggling to leave their countries for greener pastures. If they are refused visas to travel abroad, some end up developing hypertension. Evangelists would have been out of business if the same efforts many people make to get out of their countries like in Nigeria where I live is applied to seek the kingdom of God. If you ask me of the class of such people, I would say they are simply chicken.

A CALL FOR IMMEDIATE ACTION

Many points in this course book are summarized in the ten guidelines for success given by Marshal Field. He said:

(1) The value of time - don't waste it
(2) The value of perseverance - don't give up.
(3) The pleasure of hard work - don't be lazy.
(4) The dignity of simplicity - don't be complicated
(5) The worth of character - don't be dishonest
(6) The power of kindness - don't be uncaring
(7) The call of duty - don't shun responsibility
(8) The wisdom of economy - don't be a spendthrift
(9) The virtue of patience - don't be impatient
(10) The improvement of skill - don't stop practicing.

And I will add this: The eternal value of salvation - do everything to keep it.

Having gone through this course, you can now begin to take action. It is not enough to learn all the principles of success as a Christian. You must put them into practice. Do not think of the time you will spend to reach your goal. A thousand mile journey begins with a step. Start the journey from where you are. Read the book over and over again if that will make you fully digest the contents of the course. I love people going into action. The best help you can get anywhere in the world is the one you are ready to offer yourself. I do hope the little I have rendered in this course book is good enough to help you. Like someone said, "a chicken in Nigeria is a chicken in America, the so-called land of opportunities. An eagle in Nigeria is an eagle in Europe and anywhere else."

Be an eagle and stay an eagle wherever you are. If you remain a chicken, you risk falling prey of the hawk that flies everywhere. Do not be a hawk that risks being shot down by the hunter (the law). Be an

69

eagle that has nothing to worry about even though the world is full of evils because of your ability as a Christian to soar in the environment you have chosen to stay. The Bible says in Isaiah 40: 31, *'But they that wait upon the Lord shall renew their strengths; they shall mount up with wings as eagles; they shall run, and not be weary; and they shall walk, and not faint.'*

Work, pray and wait until the time God will give you the success you have been looking for.

DELIVERANCE METHODOLOGY

(BOOK FOUR)

INTRODUCTION

A critical study of so many events all over the world reveals the fact that many people blame the devil for their problems. Though everybody, including Christians can be assumed to need deliverance from one thing or the other but not from the same sources or the same methods. The Bible says in Psalm 34:19, *"Many are the afflictions of the righteous: but the Lord delivered him out of them all."* According to this passage, the righteous people really need deliverance from things that bring about afflictions. The story of Joseph in Genesis, from chapter 37 to chapter 43, is a typical example of a righteous person going through afflictions as a result of visions and what he stands for.

Joseph had a vision which obviously came from God through dreams. The vision caused him to go through afflictions. He went from slavery to imprisonment for the offence he did not commit. If some of the ministers of modern days were to be his pastors, they would have concluded that some demons were after him in the double. He actually needed deliverance but not from demons as some people would have thought. He needed deliverance from afflictions that was attributed to the vision God has given him.

At the appointed time, the vision came to fulfilment. He was delivered and he became what God ordained him to be.

Another classic example which is found in Exodus 3:1-10 is the story of the Israelites in the land of Egypt, the land of bondage. They needed deliverance from Pharaoh. So God sent Moses to deliver them. God promised them a land flowing with milk and honey but He never told them the price that went along with it. When they could not get what they bargained for in the wilderness, they contemplated going back to Egypt Deuteronomy 1:19-32. Since God would not allow that, He dealt with them in a hard way. It is instructive to note two things in this story. They are:

(i) It is one thing to know one needs deliverance and it is another thing to know how to go about it.

(ii) No matter the type of deliverance a person is looking for, there is always a price to be paid. Such price may come in form of sacrifice, patience, endurance or obedience.

Unknown to many people, everybody in this world, including Christians constantly needs deliverance from one thing or the other. As long as we live, we will always need deliverance from many things.

That is why we recite the Lord's Prayer in Matthew 6:9-13. Before we can appreciate this fact, however, there is need to understand what deliverance is all about.

WHAT IS DELIVERANCE

Although this subject is not really a theological or academic issue but we need to consider the literal meaning of deliverance. According to Oxford Dictionary, deliverance means rescue or being set free. Another dictionary defined it as the act of saving from harm or danger, or the state of being saved. The scriptural meaning is about the same thing, especially if we consider the mission of our Lord Jesus Christ on earth. Before we consider Jesus as the deliverer, there is need to consider deliverers in the book of Judges. In chapter four of the book, Deborah, the prophetess was used to deliver Israel from Sisera. In chapter six to eight we see how God used Gideon to deliver the same people from the hands of Midians. The list goes on like that.

If we do not need deliverance, Jesus would not have come to die for us. His death on the cross of Calvary not only brings about salvation but also deliverance from sins, sorrow and other problems. That is why people sing:

> *The blood of Jesus*
> *The blood of Jesus set me free*
> *From the sin and sorrow....*

Jesus is our Lord and Saviour. Saviour means the one that saves. To be saved is synonymous to delivered. In other words, Jesus is our Deliverer. Since Jesus is the Saviour or Deliverer, it means that He saves us from death, sins and afflictions.

Having considered what deliverance is and who the deliverer is, it is essential to consider what we need deliverance from.

The two major things every human being needs deliverance from are: sin and spirits.

SIN

The first thing everyone in this world needs deliverance from is sin. If sin is not removed from his life, nothing about his life would be right even if he looks as if all is well.

Sin is a direct or indirect rebellion to the word of God. While Samuel was telling Saul about his sin in 1 Samuel 15:23, he said, *"For rebellion is as the sin of witchcraft, and stubbornness is as iniquity and idolatry..."* Sin can also be omission to do what is right according to James 4:17 which says, *"Therefore to him that knows to do good and*

73

does it not, to him it is a sin." This probably confirms what Edmund Burke said. He said, *"The only thing necessary for the triumph of evil is for good men to do nothing."*

The followings are the reasons everybody needs deliverance from sin:

(i) Sin kill eternally. In Romans 6:23, the Bible says, *"For the wages of sin is death; but the gift of God is eternal life through Jesus Christ our Lord."* By nature and practice, we are all born sinners. So we need deliverance from sin since it brings eternal death as found in the book of Revelation 21:8 The passage says, *"But the fearful, and unbelieving, and abominable, and murderers, and fornicators, and idolaters, and all liars, shall have their part in the lake which burns with fire and brimstone: which is the second death."* In Ezekiel 18:20, the word of God says, *"the soul that sins, it shall die. The son shall not bear the iniquity of the father, neither shall the father bear the iniquity of the son: the righteousness of the righteous shall upon him, and the wickedness of the wicked shall be upon him."*

(ii) Sin stops God from hearing prayers. In the book of Isaiah 59:1-2, the Bible says, *"Behold, the Lord's hand is not shortened, that it cannot save; neither his ear dull, that it cannot hear: But your iniquities have separated you and your God, and yours sins have hid his face from you that he will not hear."*

(iii) Sin removes God's protection over a person and makes him vulnerable to the attack of the enemy. In 1 Peter 5:8, the Bible says, *"Be sober, be vigilant; because your adversary the devil, as a roaring lion, walks about, seeking whom he may devour."*

To get deliverance from sins, the followings steps must be taken.

(i) The person must be born again by accepting Jesus Christ as his Lord and Saviour if he wants to be saved or delivered from eternal destruction.(John3:3) If he is a backslided Christian, he needs to go back to the Lord and ask for forgiveness like the case of a prodigal son in Luke 15:11-24.

(ii) He must meditate and obey the word of God. In Psalm 119:8-11, the Bible says, *"I will keep your statutes: O forsake me not utterly. How shall a young man cleanse his way? By taking heed thereto according to your word. With my whole heart have I sought you: O let me not wander from your commandments. Your word have I hid in my heart, that I might not sin against you."*

(ii) He must abide in Christ, no matter what comes his way. In 1John3:6, the Bible says, *"Whosoever abide in him does not sin.*

Whoever sins has neither seen him nor known him."

THE SPIRITS

Many Christians, especially students of demonology lay so much emphasis on names of demons and other things that bear little or no relevance to the real issue of deliverance. For the simple purpose of this subject, we shall talk about the three types of spirits and their operations. This will help in understanding deliverance from spirits of bondage.

In Romans 8:14-16, we see the three types of spirits in the passage. It says, *"For as many as are led by the Spirit of God, they are the sons of God. For you have not received the spirit of bondage again to fear; but you have received the Spirit of adoption, by whom we cry, Abba, Father. The Spirit himself bears witness with our spirit, that we are the children of God."* Here we see that there is Spirit of God, the spirit of man and the spirits of bondage which are also called devils, demons, unclean or evil spirits.

<u>The Spirit Of God:</u> In Acts 1:8, Jesus said to His disciples, *"But you shall receive power, after the Holy Spirit has come upon you: and you shall be witnesses unto me..."* This passage established the fact that the Holy Spirit Who is the Spirit of God is the source of power of every Christian and he is to direct them in the way he should live his life.

The Spirit of God can never contract the Word of God while leading or talking to anyone about anything in anyway. In 1 Thessalonians 5:21, the Bible says, *"Test all things; hold fast that which is good."*

Some years ago, a brother came to me one day and told me that he felt that the Spirit of God wanted him to divorce his wife because she was a witch. I told him that was not the Spirit of God talking to him but the spirit of bondage. He still went ahead and divorced the wife after years of fruitful marriage. The brother went into bondage that made life miserable for him and his innocent child.

The Spirit of God can never operate in a sinful life. (Ephesians 4:22-32.) In 1 Thessalonians 5:19, the Bible says, *"Quench not the Spirit."* Even if a person is filled with the Spirit of God, the moment he begins to commit sins, the presence of the Spirit of God begins to cease if he does not repent. A deliverance minister who was so anointed that witches and wizards feared him touched the private part of one his female Church members who went to him for prayers. That act made the Spirit of God to depart from him, exposing him to demons he once tormented. The man is now dead.

The Spirit of God makes it possible for Christian to walk in the Spirit and exhibit the fruits of the Spirit, according to Galatians 5:16-23.

The Spirit Of Man: To understand the concept of the spirit of man, it is necessary to briefly study the anatomy (the whole three parts) of a total person. This study will take us to the book of Genesis 1:26 where God said to Himself, being Three in One (God; The Father, God; The Son and God The Holy Spirit as in Matthew 28;19), *"Let us make man in Our image, according to Our likeness."* One of the things man has in common with God is that man is tripartite. Man has body, spirit and soul. When God was about to make man in Genesis 2:7, He made his body from the dust of the ground and gave him a soul. According to that passage, it was after God breathed through his nostrils that man became a living soul. In other words, the breath of life from God becomes the spirit of man. Consider the diagram below as a sketch of anatomy of a total man.

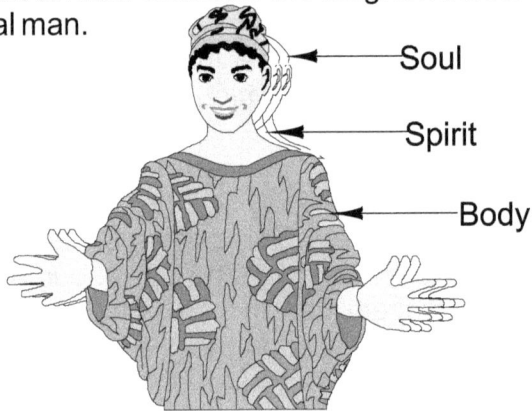

Soul

Spirit

Body

The body which is the only physical or visible part of man is linked with the soul by the spirit. The spirit is like the rope that joins the body and the soul together. Thus man cannot die. However, when the breathe of God (the spirit of man) leaves the body, the soul will have to depart from the world to face judgment, according to Hebrew 9:27 while the body goes back into the dust, according to Genesis 3:19. What man calls death is actually sleep, according to 1 Thessalonians 4:23-14. Real deaths are two types, which are spiritual and eternal. Spiritual death is when a man is disconnected from God, the real source of his life. Jesus is sent to the world as the Way to the Father in heaven, The truth about life and the Saviour that brings spiritually dead man back to life, according to John 14:6. Coincidentally, the enemy of mankind also has three missions against mankind, according to what Jesus said in John 10:10. They are: to steal the body of man and use it to sin against God, kill him spiritually by making him ignorant of the real source of life and to destroy his soul in hell. This aspect of the missions of the devil will treated later.

In Revelation 21:8, the Bible says, *"But the fearful, and unbelieving, and the abominable, and murderers, and whoremongers, and sorcerers, and idolaters, and all liars, shall have their part in the lake which burneth with fire and brimstone: which is the second death."*

The above passage leads to the study of eternal death, which is called the second death. A person dies the second time in hell if he is spiritually dead. A spiritually death person is the one without Jesus Christ as his Lord and Saviour.

Having studied the anatomy of the total man, there is need to study the functions of spirit of man. They are as follows:

1. Man glorifies God with his spirit and body, according to 1 Corinthians 6:20, which says, *"For you are bought with a price; therefore glorify God in your body and in your spirit, which are God's."*
2. With his spirit, a person believes the word of God. (2 Corinthians 4:13-14).
3. Believers also operates in the spirit realm with their spirits (Revelation 1:10).
4. Man worship God with his spirit, according to John 4:23.

The Spirit Of Bondage: The spirits of bondage are the evil spirits that put people into bondage, having three missions above. We are going to lay more emphasis on these spirits because everybody, including Christians needs deliverance from these spirits. They operate through three major ways. These are (i) Depressions (ii) Oppressions and (iii) Possessions.

DEPRESSION

In Proverb 12:25, the Bible says, *"Anxiety in the heart of man causes depression, But a good work makes it glad."* From this passage, we can see the spirit of bondage using anxieties in various ways to depress people. This can bring about bad habits or negative thoughts which ushers a person into oppressions.

Everybody is having one form of bad habit or negative thought or the other which depresses him. Some people had been so influenced by situations in life or by their environments that they have developed some bad habits or attitudes. As it is natural for a person to be influenced by things he can perceive with any of his senses in his environment, all human beings need serious and constant deliverance from negative influences that creep into their minds through the eyes, ears, noses, mouths and skins. The spirits of bondage have used all these areas to either depress or oppress or possess everybody, including Christians, using means of entertainments like songs and movies, education and media to influence their thoughts and habits.

Some of the bad habits and negative thoughts are found in 1Timothy 4:1-3 and 2Timothy 3:2-7 which may include doubt, deception, heresies, selfishness, lies, pride, love of money, discriminations, religious conflicts, disunity, lack of love, hopelessness, idle mind, laziness, covetousness, hypocrisies, doubt, unbelief, belief in one's knowledge and other negative attitudes. The list is endless. No one can claim that he is not haunted or disturbed by one bad habit and negative thought or the other.

The higher a person goes in Christianity, the more he discovers that he constantly needs deliverance from some negative thoughts and habits. If the devil cannot get ways to influence his attitudes, he knows how to depress him through negative thoughts. He can use people to stir up his emotional feelings and scheme situations to provoke him to take certain steps that will give people reasons to question his Christian faith.

Many people who are oppressed by spirit of bondage are first depressed. If they lack knowledge of what to do, they are further possessed by unholy spirits by tempting them to go places they are not supposed to go, do things they are not supposed to do and or associate with people they are supposed to avoid.

The same methods of deliverance that can be applied under depression are found under oppressions and possessions.

OPPRESSIONS

In Psalm 119:134, David prayed, *"Redeem me from oppression of man, that I may keep Your precepts."* This passage indicates that David understood that oppression can lead to moving away from God's precepts. In other words, the spirits of bondage can use human beings to oppress the others with the aim of putting them into bondage.

In 2 Corinthians 4:8-9, the Bible says, *"We (Christians) hard-pressed on every side, yet not crushed; we are perplexed, but not in despair; persecuted, but not forsaken; struck down, but not destroyed."* Thus oppression can simply be defined as an act of making someone feel uncomfortable, perplexed, persecuted, sick or fed up with life. While righteous people may not be possessed with spirits of bondage, they can be oppressed by them. A typical example of a righteous person who is oppressed in the Bible is Job. In Job 1: 8, the Bible says, *"And the LORD said unto Satan, Have you considered my servant Job, that there is none like him in the earth, a blameless* and an upright man, one that fears God, and turns away from evil?" If God can still allow the devil to deal ruthlessly with Job in spite of his confirmed stand with Him, it follows therefore that there is no one the devil cannot oppress. It is of little wonder Jesus, while teaching his disciples how to pray, taught them to always ask the Lord to deliver them from evil in Matthew 6:13.

Oppressions can come in three major ways which are (i) Affliction/Sickness (ii) Problems/Sufferings (iii) Tribulations.

Affliction/Sickness: In James 5:13-14, the Bible says, *"Is any afflicted among you? Let him pray. Is any merry? Let him sing Psalms. Is any sick among you? Let him call for the elders of the Church; and let them pray over him, anointing him with oil in the name of the Lord."* When a person is afflicted or sick, it could be an oppression from the spirits of bondage as in the case of Job.

Problems/Sufferings: In 1 Peter 4:12-13, the Bible says, *"Beloved, think it not strange concerning the fiery trial which is to test you, as though some strange thing happened unto you: But rejoice, since you are partakers of Christ's suffering; that, when his glory shall be revealed, you may be glad also with exceeding joy."* Most Christians are going through problems and sufferings which are actually oppressions of the spirits of bondage because they are followers of Jesus. According to the above passage, problems and sufferings of Christians are not strange phenomenons. There is no level a person can get to in Christian life that he would not face problems. For every level you get to, there is a new devil waiting to remind you that as long as you are in this world, you are not free from his oppressions.

Tribulations: In Romans 8:35-36, the Bible says, *"Who shall separate us from the love of Christ? Shall tribulation, or distress, or persecution, or famine, or nakedness, or peril, or sword? As it is written, For your sake we are killed all the day long; we are accounted as sheep foe the slaughter."*

Christians also go through so much tribulations that without grace of God, the spirits of bondage can make them compromise and then turn them into slaves or vessels, which the devil or demons can begin to use.

Even though oppressions come from the devil, only God or the person who is oppressed can give him the approval or the chance to oppress him.

There are some reasons God allows His people to go through oppressions of the devil. In Deuteronomy 8:2-3, Moses said, while explaining why the people of Israel have to go through wilderness before they can possess the promised land, *"And you shall remember all the way which the LORD your God led you these forty years in the wilderness, to humble you, and to test you, to know what is in your heart, whether you would keep his commandments, or not. And he humbled you, and allowed you to hunger, and fed you with manna, which you knew not, neither did your fathers know; that he might make you know that man does not live by bread only, but by every word that proceeds out of the mouth of the LORD does man live."*

The following reasons God permits some problems that seem like oppression can be inferred from the passage. These are:

(i) It is to test or make the oppressed person prove to everyone including the devil that nothing can remove his love for God as in the case of Job. The love of a person can be best proven through his obedience to God in spite of the oppression of the devil.

(ii) It is to make a person humble and remind him that he is nothing without God as in the case of Nebuchadnezzar who became so powerful that he boasted in Daniel 4:30, *"...Is not this great Babylon, that I have built for the house of the honour of my majesty?"* In verses 31 to 33, the Bible says, *"While the word was in the king's mouth, there fell a voice from heaven, saying, O king Nebuchadnezzar, to you it is spoken; The kingdom has departed from you. And they shall drive you from men, and your dwelling shall be with the beasts of the field; they shall make you eat grass like oxen, and seven times shall pass over you, until you know that the most High rules in the kingdom of men, and gives it to whomever he will. The same hour was the thing fulfilled upon Nebuchadnezzar; and he was driven from men and did eat grass like oxen, and his body was wet with the dew of heaven, till his hair had grown like the eagles' feathers, and his nails like a birds' claw."*

From the above passage, we can see that some people would not appreciate what God has done for them if the devil does not oppress then. Many people like Nebuchabnezzar would never recognize God in their lives if things are so rosy for them.

There was a time I went to share the word of God with a rich man. The first question he asked was, "why must I accept Jesus in my life? I don't have any problem like most of you, Christians. I have good health and I don't lack anything." I shook my head and asked God in my quiet prayer to prove it to him that he needed God more than anything or anyone. About three months later, he sent someone to look for me. He has lost his good health and he wished God will take all his money and give him back his good health. He made a vow that he would live his life for God if He restored his health. God granted him the request after we prayed. From that day, he knew God is the source of everything about his life.

(iii) God also allows the devil to oppress a person if He wants to get his attention as in the case of the rich man or to make him draw closer to Him in holiness, prayers and fasting. In Psalms 35:10-13, the Bible says, *"All my bones shall say, LORD, who is like unto you, who delivers the poor from him that is too strong for him, yea, the poor and the needy that plunders him? False witnesses did rise up; they laid to my charge things that I knew not. They rewarded me with evil for good to the sorrow of my soul. But as for me, when they were sick, my clothing was sackcloth: I humbled my soul with fasting; and my prayers returned into my bosom."*

It must be noted that not all oppressions of the devil are allowed by God. In fact most of the oppressions are actually caused by the people that are being oppressed. The avenues through which the devil gains access to oppress people are many. We shall discuss the commonest ways which are as follows: (i) Un-repented sin (ii) Unbroken covenant with spirits of bondage (iii) Disobedience to God (iv) Bad counseling/ Bad influence (v) Ignorance (vi) Spirit Of Fear.

Un-repented Sin: In Romans 6:12-23, the Bible explains the consequence of sins. In verse 12, we read, *"Let not sin therefore reign in your mortal body, that you should obey it in its lust."* In verse 16, the Bible says, *"Know you not, that to whom you yield yourselves servants to obey; whether sin unto death, or of obedience unto righteousness?"* This indicates that sin gives room for the spirits of bondage to operate in the live of a person and also kills eternally. The devil will never leave some people alone, no matter how much they pray for deliverance because of their sinful ways of life are not changed.

A minister conducted a deliverance session for a man who got delivered from the spirit epilepsy. Few days later the spirit came back and tormented him the more. The minister conducted deliverance again. The spirit left and came back again. Later, the minister counseled the man, trying to find out where things went wrong. He discovered that each time the man got delivered, he went to commit fornication.

Un-repented sin is a very good ground for spirits of bondage to oppress or destroy anyone.

Unbroken Covenant With Spirit Of Bondage: Some people who are not be oppressed through un-repented sin may be oppressed through unbroken covenant they or their families have entered into

81

with unclean spirits. In Deuteronomy 5:1-10, Moses reminded the people of Israel of the covenant they made with God in verses 7, and 9, *"You shall have none other gods before me...You shall not bow down yourself unto them, nor serve them: for I the LORD your God is a jealous God, visiting the iniquity of the fathers upon the children unto the third and forth generation of them that hate me."*

Nigeria went through so much oppressions, especially during the military regime because the nation was involved in idolatry in the disguise of African cultures in 1977. The nation spent fortunes that were realized from the natural resources. Various idols were brought from many countries to be celebrated. Few years later, Nigeria began to experience serious oppressions that extend to the people that were not born at that time up till this time.

Covenant with spirits of bondage can be broken through prayers and humility before God. In 2 Chronicles 7:14, the Bible says, *"If my people, who are called by my name, shall humble themselves, and pray, and seek my face, and turn from their wicked ways; then will I hear from heaven, and will forgive their sin, and will heal their land."*

Disobedience To God: This can happen in two ways. One of the ways is to disobey the word of God which everybody is expected to obey as it is written in the scriptures. For instance, the Bible says in Romans 12:2, *"And be not conformed to this world: but be transformed by the renewing of your mind, that you may prove what is that good, and acceptable, and perfect will of God."* Everybody is expected to obey that simple commandment come what may. The violation of that instruction leads to sin. This can give spirit of bondage a chance to operate.

The other way is to disobey the instruction that is specifically given to a person. Take for example the case of Jonah who was instructed by God in Jonah 1:1-17 to go to Nineveh. He ran to Tarshish where he got himself and others into trouble with storm. The storm threatened to overthrow their ship. The people never got deliverance from the storm until Jonah was thrown into the sea where he was swallowed by a great fish. The fish took him to the place God sent him. Similarly, if God tells a person to go to a particular place and he disobeys, that will amount to disobedience. This will give the spirit of bondage the chance to oppress the person or use the situation against him.

I counseled a lady who was planning to get married a few years ago. I asked her how the Lord told her she should go about it. She said He wanted her to do it quietly but her plan was too elaborate for a quiet wedding. She has printed wedding invitations in hundreds and yet she wanted a quiet wedding. I made her realized that she was not planning a quiet wedding and if she went contrary to what she was told, she would be looking for trouble. She argued that that was how others did theirs, forgetting the fact that God gave a specific instruction about her wedding for the reason best known to Him. She did it as she wanted it and gave the enemy the chance to come into her marriage. The marriage did not yield any fruit. Instead it was constant quarrel and sorrow until a minister from another town came to hold a crusade in the church. The word of knowledge came to the man and he declared that some fetish items had been planted into her marriage through a wall clock that was presented to the couple on their wedding day. The couple got their deliverance but that was after about five years of oppressions of the devil.

If a person is obedient to God in everything, there is no way the devil will get the chance to oppress him although, this does not mean he would not be afflicted. If he is faced with affliction, the purpose of that affliction is to promote him like the case of Joseph who moved from his family into slavery; from slavery into prison; from prison to the throne.

Bad Counseling/ Bad Influence: Many people have gotten into bondage of the devil through bad counseling or bad influence of others. The Bible says in Proverb 19:27, *"Cease, my son, to hear the instruction that causes to stray from the words of knowledge."* Bad influence comes through teachers, ministers or advisers that lack knowledge of the word of God in their lives. This group of people had been in existence for so long and, whether we like it or not, they will continue to exist. In Romans 2:20-23, the Bible talks of instructor of the foolish and teacher of babies who could not teach themselves and yet they want to influence others. They want to teach others how to be rich yet they are poor. They want to teach others about holiness yet they are far from being holy. Such people even head a Church.

I have seen such people with bad influence fighting over the tithes of their Church members. These people will mount the pulpit and preach eloquent messages that appeal only to the intellect of the people instead of their spirits. Anyone who submits the control of his soul to such person gives the spirit of bondage room to operate in his or her life.

Bad influence also comes through the doctrines of the devil. In 1Timothy 4:1, the Bible says, *"Now the Spirit speaks expressly, that in the latter times some shall depart from faith, giving heed to deceitful spirits, and doctrines of demons."* The reason the spirits of the devil introduce various doctrines is mainly to attack the faith of the people of

God. The devil uses so many things to establish his doctrines even right in the Church. These include (i) the people he has ordained *or* anointed as his workers everywhere (ii) Ungodly publications (iii) Movies or Television programs (iii) Internet and (iv) Radio.

By using every means available to reach the people with his doctrines, the devil seeks to gain access into the lives of those that give him the chance. He does not only plan to oppress the people but to possess and destroy them eternally.

To get deliverance from bad counseling and bad influence, including doctrine of the devil, people need to do the followings:

(i) Keep the word of God in their hearts (Psalm 119:9-12). The devil would not strike a person without first taking the word of God from him, which is the sword of the Spirit, according to Ephesians 6:17.

(ii) Avoid bad company and negative influence or friendship. (1 Corinthians 15:33, Psalm 1:1-6)

(iii) Seek only godly instructions. In Proverb 28:9, the Bible says, *"He that turns away his ear from hearing the law, even his prayer shall be abomination."* In other words, if anyone refuses to accept the word of God as a way of life and direction, his prayers will irritate God and that is enough to allow the spirits of bondage to oppress him.

Ignorance: In Hosea 4:6, God says: *"My people perish for lack of knowledge..."* As Myles Munroe put it, while explaining the passage, the people do not perish because the devil destroys them, not because of sin but because they lack knowledge. Many things are going wrong in the lives of so many people because they lack the knowledge of the word of God. Thus they need deliverance from ignorance. If a person wants to attack an enemy without information about his strength, he may be going on a suicide mission. If a person does not know much about the business he is about to do, he will likely to go bankrupt and then blame the devil for it.

Ignorance is a very destructive weapon which the spirits of bondage can use to oppress anybody, however anointed.

Spirit Of Fear: In 2 Timothy 1:7, the bible says, *"For God has not given us the spirit of fear; but of power, and of love, and of sound mind."* The spirit of fear, according to this passage is capable of:

(i) destroying power of God in the life of everybody, including Christians if it is given the chance. This power, which makes a person a child of God through faith in Jesus Christ, according John 1:12, can be threatened by the spirit of fear. It always prevents many Christians from taking steps which they are supposed to take. It shuts their mouths up when they are supposed to talk. It also makes Christians compromise when they are supposed to stand by what they believe. Whatever a man fears, he empowers.

(ii) It kills the potentials of Spirit of love in a Christian by introducing doubts in the love of God for him, tormenting a person and putting his faith and trust in Jesus Christ into question. (1John 4:17-18)

(iii) It finally removes his Christian sanity by making him behave in an ungodly way or in a manner that is contrary to the word of God. (Romans 12:9-18)

The real mission of the spirit of fear is to compel a Christian to conform to the pattern of the devil or to the standard of the world. However, this spirit can be overcome through:

(A) building faith and trust in God (Hebrew 11:1-6),
(B) building courage and confidence through the word of God (Deuteronomy 31:6),
(C) Walking in the Spirit (Galatians 5:16-25) and
(D) Praying all the time (1 Thessalonians 5:17).

There are few things all humans must first understand if they do not want the devil or spirits of bondage to oppress them. These things are: (i) The Word Of God (ii) The Ways Of God and (iii) The Missions Of The Devils.

THE WORD OF GOD

No matter what had been said about the word of God, it cannot be overemphasized. The word of God specifies the way of life which must be followed before anyone can get deliverance from anything. Many people go through needless afflictions because they are ignorant of the word of God. The devil takes great advantage of the ignorance of the people, making them to walk in the way of death without them knowing it. According to John 1:1, the Word of God is Himself. In essence, anyone who does not receive the word of God actually refuses God.

In Ephesians 6:17, the Bible says that The Word of God is also the sword of the Spirit. Christians do not use only prayers to fight. They use prayers with the word of God to either deal with their problems or the devil that oppresses them. For anyone to get deliverance from the oppression of the devil, he must be fervent in the word of God - the Bible. Remember that Jesus overcame the temptations and oppressions of the devil with the word of God according to Luke 4:1-13.

THE WAYS OF GOD

In Psalms 106:42-43, the Bible says, *"Their enemies also oppressed them, and they were brought into subjection under their hand. Many times did he deliver them; but they provoked him with their counsel, and were brought low for their iniquity."*

People try to connect with their Maker through various ways. Because they are ignorant of the real way of God, they get involved in various forms of religions and some forms of worship that give spirits of bondage the chance to take over the control of their lives. The spirits often try to satisfy their yearnings for God through demonic activities and convince them that they are connected with God when they are actually in connection with some sorts of demons. The worship of these spirits may sometimes look like worship of the Almighty God. For someone who does not have the gift of discernment, the only way to know is to compare the activities of such people with the word of God and see if they are in conformity. This is the best way to prove His real way.

In Hebrew 3:10, God says, *"Therefore I was grieved with that generation, and said, They do always err in their heart; and they have not known my ways."* From that passage, it is obvious that if someone does not know the way of God, he will err. Such error can give the spirits of bondage the chance to oppress and destroy him.

Jesus said in John 14:6, *"I am the way, the truth, and the life: no man comes to the Father, but by me."* It follows therefore that nothing can be right with anyone who has not accepted Jesus Christ in his life. If people pray for him, he may get deliverance but it will be short-lived if Christ does not live in his life.

There was a barren woman who was a Muslim. We worked together as civil servants some years ago. When she became desperate to get a child, she went to a Christian crusade. The minister specifically told her to allow Jesus, the Giver of children to come into her life if she wanted to hold unto her miracle. Not long after that, she had a baby. After getting what she wanted, she went back to her religion. A few years later, the spirits of bondage got hold of her. Her two legs became so paralyzed that she could not walk. The medical test indicated that nothing was wrong with her physically. She began to seek for Christ for solution to her problem again.

THE MISSIONS OF THE DEVIL

Jesus said in John 10:10, *"The thief comes not, but to steal, and to kill, and to destroy: I am come that they might have life, and that they might have it more abundantly."* The devil is the thief and according to this passage, the missions of the devil are (i) to steal (ii) to kill and (iii) to destroy.

Going by the implications of each mission, it is apparent that the devil pays much more attention at people of God than anyone else in the world. He ensures that people are ignorant of his missions, thereby giving him the chance to carry them out.

To steal: Since no one can steal what belongs to him, it follows therefore that the devil steals the people of God. How he does that is quite interesting. He entices them with things of the world, especially flashy things. The moment a Christian begins to lusts after things that are not given to him by God, he moves towards becoming the enemy of God. Once they become the enemies of God, he uses these very things to control their lives. That is why a man who is making so money will never indicate that he had made enough. The Bible says in 1 John 2:15, *"Love not the world, neither the things that are in the world. If any man loves the world, the love of the Father is not in him."*

Many Christians had been taken away from God and yet they believe they belong to God. If you want to know those who are ignorant of this area of the mission of the devil, check their attitudes towards things of the world.

To kill: I would like to illustrate this mission with the story of a man who goes to the bush, holding a gun and killing as many animals he sees around. He has a big bag where he keeps the animals he has killed. Not bordering himself about the dead ones in the bag, he goes after the ones that are going about carelessly. In the same manner, the devil will never border himself about the spiritually dead people because they are food for him anytime of the day. He would therefore concentrate his efforts on those who are alive spiritually. According to 1 John 2:16-17, the things which the devil uses as weapons to kill people spiritually include the lust of the flesh; the lust of the eyes and the pride of life:

(a) **Lust of the flesh**: The works of the flesh are so much and so forceful that Christians constantly need deliverance from them. In Galatians 5:19-21, the Bible lists the works of the flesh which the devil uses to fight against people of God. The most rampant of the lust of flesh among the people that professed to be Christians are fornication and adultery. There are far so many Christians, including their leaders dying spiritually through this way. The devil deceives them by saying it does not matter, especially if it is just once but the truth is that he needs that just "once" to gain access into the life of that person before he kills him spiritually. Unknown to many people, the sins of adultery and fornication has far more spiritual damage in the life of a person than anyone can imagine it. It is like the case of a healthy person who takes delicious but poisonous food that destroys the body system. If he takes a bit, it will take him months of serious medical treatments before he can recover. Even if he recovers, the scars will still be in the body, making him weaker than what he used to be. It is the same with someone who is once spiritually strong, committing adultery or fornication. The principle of "prevention is better than cure" in medical term is much more applicable to spiritual life. If a Christian, however strong or healthy, goes into sexual sin, he begins to die gradually though he may still appear like a good Christian. Once he is dead, according to the story about the hunter, the devil pays little or no attention to him.

(b) **The lust of the eyes**: This is another way of killing people of God spiritually. This can be treated as an act of covetousness and love of money. Money seems to give many people security and comfort. Thus they are not contended with what God has given them, no matter how much. To make the matter more critical, many preachers are fond of preaching prosperity messages that make the people more determined to possess more of things of this world. I know of a man who had been filled with this kind of messages that the teachings about holiness and sacrifice of personal convenience for the benefit of other are strange to him. He told me that God would never allow modern Christians to suffer like the early Christians. I asked him why he thought like that. He said the early Christians were not under the grace like the present ones. The modern Christians, according to him, were to enjoy what the early Christians had done. That is exactly the way the devil wants every Christian to think or feel. When God begins to deal with them, they will lose faith and then turn away from Him, making them to sacrifice things of eternal values for temporal things and vanities. In 1Timothy 6:7-12, the Bible says, *"For we brought nothing into this world and it is certain we can carry nothing out. And having food and clothing let us be contended with these things. But they that will be rich fall into temptation and a snare, and into many foolish and hurtful lusts, which plunge men into destruction and perdition. For the love of money is the root of all evil: which while some coveted after, they have erred from faith, and pieced themselves through with many sorrows. But you, O man of God, flee these things; and follow after righteousness, godliness, faith, love, patience, meekness. Fight the* *good fight of faith, lay hold on eternal life, to which you are also called, and have professed a good profession before many witnesses."* Christians are warned in the above passage of the effect of covetousness and the love of money. The devil has a way of using the eyes of the people to see the glory of the world and tries constantly to make them do anything to possess it. That is why some people can go as far as going into shady businesses, dishonesty, corruption and even fraud. This is not a new trick of the devil. He used it to take the dominion from Adam through Eve in Genesis 3:1-6. He tried to use it to make Jesus surrender His Lordship to him in Matthew 4:1-10. In verses 8 and 9, the Bible says, *"Again, the devil took him up into an exceedingly high mountain, and showed him all the kingdoms of the world, and the glory of them; And said unto him, All these things will I give you, if you fall down and worship me."* The devil successfully uses the same old method to trick people of God. People worship not only the devil but also human beings like them because of the vain glory of the world which they can perceive with their eyes.

(c) **The Pride Of Life**: This spirit of pride of life has different faces, which often take the form of self confidence, feeling of superiority over others or thought of having so much knowledge about life. It can also be in the form of taking pride in a person's social status or family background, making him more conscious of whom he is in the world than the person who is save through grace of God in Jesus Christ. In Romans 12:3, the Bible says, *"For I say, through the grace given unto me, to every man that is among you, not to think of himself more highly than he ought to think; but to think soberly, according as God has dealt to every man in measure of faith."* We can see that much knowledge about things of this world can ensnare a soul but there is no way a person can have too much knowledge about Almighty God who is to great for anyone because of man's limited brain capacity.

The face of spirit of pride of life is also praising oneself as it is seen in Proverb 27:2. Trusting in one's ability rather than God is another form of pride of life (Proverb 3:5). There are so many attributes of pride of life. Sometimes, it is difficult to notice, especially when everybody has got something to be proud of. As minor as this spirit may seem, it is an ideal weapon for the devil to kill easily. A spiritually alive person is always clothed with humility which is the only thing that can be used to destroy pride of life. In John 13:13-14, Jesus said to His disciples, *"You call me Teacher and Lord: and you say rightly;*

89

for so I am. If then, I your Lord and Teacher, have washed your feet; you also ought to wash one another's feet." The washing of feet is symbolic. It means ability to stoop low and do humble things for one another.

I remember the time the Lord stripped me of so many things in my ministries. He commanded me to go to a town and handle children in one big Church that never seem to appreciate my service. I would be the one to clean the hall we normally use as the children Church. I had no worker and no encouragement from anyone. I sat down one Sunday and thought of my ministry that was doing great and suddenly asked myself, "why must I do this minor work? This is not what I am trained for!" The Spirit of God said to me, "if you are too big to do that minor work, then your are actually too small to do any work with Me." I repented immediately. Since that day, I took special delight in doing any work for the Lord. The Bible says in Proverb 16:18, *"Pride goes before destruction, and a haughty spirit before a fall."*

To destroy: This is the concluding part of the mission of the devil in the life of a person. Destruction in this case means eternal destruction in hell. A person cannot be destroyed when he is still alive physically because he still has the chance to accept Jesus Christ Who gives eternal life. In John 3:16, the Bible says, *"For God so love the world, that he gave his only begotten Son, that whosoever believes in him should not perish, but have everlasting life."* The word "perish" there means eternal destruction. Destruction is described as second death in hell in Revelation 21:8: *"But the fearful, and the unbelieving, and the abominable, and murderers, and fornicators, and sorcerers, and idolaters, and all liars, shall have their part in the lake which burns with fire and brimstone: which is the second death."*

With this, we conclude the aspect of oppression of spirits of bondage and now move to the area of depression.

POSSESSIONS

There is a case study in Matthew 8:28-32 which explains the condition of a possessed person. When the spirits of bondage that possessed the man in the story was cast away, the demons needed a place to stay. Jesus sent them to the herd of swine as they requested. The possessed person became well but the swine perished. In other words, the ultimate goal of the demons was to lead the man into total destruction. Possession can, therefore, be defined as an act of inhabiting or owning or controlling something by legal or illegal means. Evil spirits can inhabit or live inside people, especially these who are not filled with the Spirit of God.

Spirits of bondage operate in the lives of their hosts (the possessed persons) even though they do not have the right to dwell inside them. Their hosts or those who have the spiritual or legal authority over them, however, give them chance to possess them. There is hardly anyone who is not possessed with either the Spirit of God or spirits of bondage. A person who is not possessed with Spirit of God would be possessed with spirits of bondage like spirit of witchcraft, sorcery, violence, stealing, fear, anger, lust or the like.

Some years ago, I preached in the Church where I was the pastor and asked everyone who needed counsel to wait behind to see me. There was a youth who confessed to me that she used to steal even though she tried all she could to stop. With prayers, counseling and determination on her part, she was delivered from the spirit of stealing.

By possessing a person, the spirit of bondage, takes over his life completely. He cannot operate his free wills. Hence, some of them behave like mad people and some slept with any man or woman like street dogs. The bodies of possessed people had been stolen from them and now serve as the vessels of the thief - the devil. Possessed people can be made to walk round the street naked and behave in an unnatural way without them feeling any qualms about that.

Some years ago, I was taking a walk down the street in Nigeria when I came across a seemingly mad woman, holding a heavy looking club with the intention to strike an old man with it. Nobody could rescue him from her as it was obvious that she was insane and violent enough to strike anybody dead. I went to the woman despite the people's warning that I could be struck with the club. I made sure that the woman looked at me in the face before I commanded her to hand over the club to me. Inwardly, I prayed that God should make her yield to me in the Name of Jesus. The people were stunned when the woman gave me the club and went on her kneels, apologizing for the wrong thing she tried to do.

Spirits of bondage gain entrance to the lives of people through these major ways that are categorized into (i) Sin (ii) Curses (iii) Invitations.

Sin: Most of all the spirits of bondage that trouble people all over the world gained access into their lives through sins which they committed or sins of their fore parents. The enemy of souls of men first gained control over this world through the sin of disobedience that was committed by Adam and Eve in the Garden of Eden in Genesis Chapter 3. Since then, everybody began to inherit burden of sins through their parents. This always takes their tolls on them. In

Jeremiah 31:29, the Bible says, *"... The fathers have eaten sour grapes, And the children's teeth are set on edge."* In other words, the fathers committed sins but the children are also bearing the consequence of sins.

Curses: Curses can be described scripturally as (i) The pronouncement of evil upon people either by God as recorded in Deuteronomy 28:15-68 or by man as in Numbers 14:1-28. (ii) Confession of evil upon oneself or another person. The people of Israel while reacting to the news that was brought to them by the men that went to spy the land of Canaan, murmured in Numbers 14:2 and 3 *"...Would God that we have died in the land of Egypt! Or would God we had died in this wilderness. And why has the LORD brought us unto this land, to fall by the sword, that our wives and children should be a prey? Were it not better for us to return into Egypt?"* The people got a reply from the Lord in verse 28 which says, *"Say unto them, As truly as I live, says the LORD, as you have spoken in my ears, so will I do to you."* All the people that made the evil pronouncement died in the wilderness as they have confessed.

When any evil is pronounced against anyone, the spirits of bondage are given the chance to operate in line with the evil pronouncement. Unless the person who is cursed is protected by the power of God, the curse may begin to operate in his life until get deliverance or until he dies.

An alliance with spirits of bondage through ignorance or worship of demons in the form of idols or customs or religions or other means can bring about curses. In Deuteronomy 32:16 and 17, the Bible says, *"They provoked Him to jealousy with strange gods, with abominations they provoked Him to anger. They sacrificed unto demons, not to God; to gods whom they knew not, to new gods that came in of late, whom your fathers feared not."* From this passage, we can see that people are ignorantly serving demons, thinking they are serving God. This set of people is different from idolaters. They may be called Christians and yet they are not. Such people may be going to Church every time and still participate in certain festivals that are directly or in directly linked with spirits of bondage.

The worship of demons which brings about curses has taken various forms in modern days. There are some customs and norms as good as they seem constitute idolatry or worship of demons. The ways some weddings, funerals, festivals and other occasions are being conducted sometimes constitute idolatry or rituals. It is a pity that so many Christians ignorantly take part in such occasions that give rooms for spirits of bondage to operate in their lives.

Invitations: There is a story the book of 1 Chronicles 4:9 and 10. It reads, *"And Jabez was more honourable than his brethren: and his mother called his name Jabez, Because I bore him in sorrow. And Jabez called on God of Israel, saying, Oh that you would bless me indeed, and enlarge my border, and your hand might be with me, and that you will keep me from evil, that it may not grieve me! And God granted him that which he requested."*

There are some things in this passage that need deep considerations. One of them is that Jabez's mother ignorantly invited the spirit of sorrow into the life of her son by calling his name Jabez which means sorrow. This gave the spirit of bondage the chance to operate in his life until he realized that he did not have to live with sorrow for the rest of his life. So he made a request of deliverance to his Maker, knowing fully well that He can deliver him and he was delivered.

Many parents ignorantly invites spirits of bondage into the lives of their children through what they confess about their children. Some may go as far as dedicating them to these spirits without realizing the serious implications of their actions in the future of the child. Their intentions may be to protect or help them succeed in life. Some like Jabez's mother called their children with the names that invite unclean spirits into their lives. I know of a woman who named her daughter Dog! And when she begins to behave like a dog, people wonder what goes wrong.

Invitations of spirits of bondage into the lives of people can be direct or indirect. It may be inherent from one generation and transferred to another. I know of a family who is under the influence the spirit of death that ensured that no member gets to the age of fifty before he or she dies. It took the power of God through a member of that family who gave her life to Christ in her late forties to break that jinx.

Having considered what we need deliverance from, we can now talk about the methods of deliverance.

METHODS OF DELIVERANCE

The method to apply in deliverance depends on who or what a person wants to be rescued from. While some people need prayers before they get deliverance, others need discipline. Some need information while some need to take some steps. Before we consider some suggested ways to get deliverance, I want us to consider the story in the Book of Acts of Apostles in Chapter 12. In that story, Peter needed deliverance from Herod, the terrible king who was out to destroy the Church. He was kept in the prison until an Angel came to deliver him. This was made possible through the prayers of some Christians at the house of Mary, the mother of John. When Peter got to the gate of the house, he needed the door of the gate to be opened. If Peter had called on the Angel to help him open the door as he did while taking him out of the prison, he would be wasting his time. The reason is that he does not need divine intervention to get the gate of the house of Mary opened. That was a job for human being. Similarly, a lot of people waste their time casting demons out of someone who merely needed to be counseled about his life.

The challenges of most people, including Christians in the area of deliverance are:

(i) They either know little or nothing about God and His ways but they know so much about the world, which invariably leads to complete ignorance about the devil that rules the world.

(ii) Some people know so much about God but know so little about the devil which leads to half knowledge and half ignorance, which invariably leads to mixing truth with lies. A lie that is hidden within the truth is more than enough to lead to bondage.

(iii) Some people think they know the truth but in truth they are deceived. Such people are the ones the Bible talks about 2Timothy 3:13, which says, *"But evil men and impostors will grow worse and worse, deceiving and being deceived."* Of course, these people are ideal tools of the spirits of bondage to deceive others and lead them in the way of destruction.

Let us now consider the major method of deliverance.

1. **_Divine Intervention:_** Most if not all cases of deliverance required divine intervention. A man who is cursed needs divine intervention before he can be delivered. There is a need to briefly talk about curses which are the problems of so many people.

Curses can be explained as confession of evil by self as in Numbers 14:1 and 2. It is also pronouncement of evil by God or man as in Deuteronomy 28:15-68. It can also mean going into covenant with devil through paying homage to him (Deuteronomy 32:17). The major cause of all types of curses which may include God-made curse, self and man made curses is simple disobedient to the word of God. As we find it in Deuteronomy 28:15 which says, *"but it shall come to pass, if you will not hearken unto the voice of the Lord your God, to observe to do all His commandments and that is statutes which I command you this day; that all these curses shall come upon you and overtake you:"* If a man curses himself through confession of evil, God can deliver him. God can also remove man-made curses or inherited curses. Simple obedience to the word of God can bring about divine intervention. The question is if God curses a man, who will deliver him? In that case he would need to plead for mercy of God. So no matter the kind of curse it may be, whether God or man-made curses or covenant with the devil, it can be broken by divine intervention.

2. **_The Word of God_:** Jesus set example of how we can get deliverance through the word of God in Matthew 4:1-11. In that passage, we see how the devil came to tempt Jesus and He deliver Himself with the word of God by saying, *"it is written…"* Some people do not really need so much prayers before they can get deliverance. All they need is to apply the word of God in their lives or situations. The word of God, according to John 1:1 is God Himself. Ephesians 6:17 makes us to understand that the word of God of the sword of the spirit. In essence we use the word of God to fight and deliver ourselves from anything we do not want. The most important thing we need for deliverance from all sorts of unpleasant things is the word of God. The word of God enlightens us on what to do in a particular situation and shed light on so many obscure things. The people the devil fear most are those who know the word of God and knows how to apply it. He knows that these people can use the word of God to deliver themselves from him and also help others to get deliverance.

Ignorance of the word of God makes so many people patronize false prophets who tell them to bring some items before they get deliverance. Simple obedience to the word of God can bring about divine intervention. Disobedience to the word of God can bring about a lot of trouble, including eternal destruction. Applying the word of God, however, can bring joy, peace, love and strengths even when the going seems so tough. Since things cannot always be smooth through out life, we all need the word of God to either deliver us or to comfort us till the end of life.

3. **_Prayer and Fasting_:** Certain deliverance requires serious prayers and even sometimes fasting as in the case of Mark 9: 17-29. At times, we need to deny ourselves certain things. Such denial, especially of food is called fasting. In the Lord's prayer in Luke 11: 1-5, we are taught to say to God, lead us not into temptation. *"Deliver us from evil…"* I Thessalonians 5:17, the Bible says, *"pray without ceasing."* The reason we have to pray without ceasing is because we constantly need deliverance from temptation or evil. In Luke 11: 6-9, Jesus used the story of a visitor who got to his friend's house at midnight. His host went to his friend to ask for food for him but was refused. His

persistence made him get what he wanted. Prayer is communing or talking with God. It is a two-way street. When you talk with someone without getting any answer, you will assume he didn't hear you or he is deaf or dumb. Since God is not deaf or dumb, He will answer if nothing is wrong with the person praying. God answers our prayers through His words or through circumstances or at times dreams. Sin hinders God from hearing a sinner, according to Psalm 66:18. In Isaiah 59: 1-2, the Bible says, *"Behold the Lord's is not shortened, that it cannot save; neither his ear heavy, that it cannot hear: But your iniquities have separated between you and your God, and your sins have hid his face from you, that he will not hear."*

Some people pray but cannot receive because, according to James 4:3, they ask amiss. Since the world is full of evils and temptations, Christians need to be prayerful if they want to be constantly delivered from them.

4. ***Praise and Worship***: A lot of people do not know the implication of not praising and worshipping God in the Church and at home as an individual, a family and Body of Christ. Christians must always praise God. When we praise and worship God, we are acknowledging Whom God is God. In Psalm 139:14, the Bible says, *"I will praise You, for I am fearfully and wonderfully made; marvelous are Your works."* When we praise and worship God even when we have problems, we are asking God to come into our situation. While prayer often takes the form of request, praise and worship to God takes the form of adoration and appreciation of Whom God is and what He has done. It is always a way of thanking God for what He has promised He would do through his word. In Acts 16: 25-26, the Bible says, *"And midnight Paul and Silas prayed, and sang praises unto God: and the prisoners heard them. And suddenly there was a great earthquake, so that the foundations of the prison were shaken; immediately the doors were opened, and everyone's band were loose."* In other words Paul and Silas were set free from prison and the chain after praising God. They got deliverance from prison through praises.

5. ***Wisdom/Good Counsel***: This kind of deliverance is needful in the kind of problem or bondage that is caused by ignorance or lack of knowledge. In 1 King 3:16-28, we see the wisdom that was displayed by Solomon when two women went to him, claiming ownership over one living child. It was a very serious case that needed wisdom of God to solve. The real mother would have probably lost the child if not for the way Solomon handled the case. On many occasions, God expects us to use the wisdom He has given us to deliver ourselves from certain

problem. If we do not have the kind of experience or wisdom to deliver ourselves from one problem, we can ask God for counsel or go to experienced people for counsel. Again, we must be careful of the kind of counsel we take from people. Some counsel can cause more harm than good. I have heard of wrong counsel destroying homes. I have seen people losing a lifetime opportunities because they were wrongly counseled. A good example of wrong counsel that can cause a whole lot of problem is found in I Kings 12:1-20. Rehoboam was given a good counsel by the elders of Israel in relation to the way he should rule the people but the Bible says that he forsook the counsel of the old men and took the foolish advice of young men like him. This made Israel to rebel against him as the heir to the throne of David and made Jeroboam the king. Wisdom and counsel of God can be a way to get deliverance from so many problems.

6. ***Change of Attitude/Habit:*** Sometimes a change of attitude or habit is the only way a person needs to get deliverance. A person who talks too much would need to discipline himself in the way he talks. All a person who wants to lose weight needs to do is to change his eating habit. A lady who is looking for a husband would need to dress like a young responsible person, not appearing like aged woman or a prostitute. Someone who needs favour of people would need to show favour to others. A person who is known with mean attitude would need to change that attitude if he wants to surround himself with kind people. The Bible says in Ezekiel 18:23-24, *"Have I any pleasure at all that the wicked should die? Says the Lord God: and not that he should live. But when the righteous turns away from his righteousness, and commits iniquity, and does according to all the abominations that the wicked man does, shall he live? All his righteousness that he had done shall not be mentioned: in his trespass that he hath trespassed and in his sin that he has sinned, in them shall he die."* We can see it from this passage that our own attitudes or habits have implications or consequences. If the attitude is positive, it has positive results. If it is negative, it has negative consequences. Any problem which is caused by attitude can only be solved by a change of attitude.

Most importantly, our attitudes according to the passage have eternal consequences. So it is better to change the attitude or habit that is opposed to the word of God.

To conclude this subject, I would say that deliverance is not restricted to one way or method but many, depending on what a person needs deliverance from.

CHRISTIANS' BASIC MINISTRIES

(BOOK FIVE)

INTRODUCTION

As a way of introducing this subject, Christian Basic Ministries, I would like to distinguish this type of servants we have in the modern days. What the word "servants" implies in this context "ministers". Since all Christians are save to serve in one capacity or the other, it implies therefore that they are all ministers in one area or the other. So many people who claim to be Christians make it difficult for others to see the differences between the various kinds of ministers that claim to be serving God. By categorizing these servants, it is not intended to criticize some ministers but rather to understand the reason Jesus will deny some people on the Day of Judgment. In Matthew 7:21-23, Jesus said, *"Not everyone that says to me, Lord, Lord, shall enter the kingdom of heaven; but he that does the will of my father which is in heaven. Many will say to me in that day, Lord, Lord, have we not prophesied in your name? and in your name have we cast out devils? And in your name have we done many wonderful works? And then I will say to them, I never knew you: depart from me, you that work iniquity."*

There are four kinds of servants but all claim to be servants or children of God. They are as follows:

Servant Of God: In 1 Corinthians 7:22, the Bible says, *"For he that is called in the Lord, being a servant, is the Lord's freeman: likewise also he that is called, being free, is Christ servant."* From this passage, we can see that all true Christians are called. They are therefore servants of God. There is a noteworthy distinction, however, between a child and a servant of God. The distinction has to do with the spiritual maturity with basic understanding of the ways of God and His words. A servant is also a child of God but he is more matured than a child who probably just comes to the knowledge of Christ or the babe that refuses to grow for whatever reason. The Bible says in Hebrew 5:13, *"For every one that uses milk is unskillful in the word of righteousness: for he is a babe."* And in 1 Peter 2:2, the Bible also says, *"As newborn babes, desire the sincere milk of the word, that ye may grow thereby."* From these passages, we can see that a newly converted Christian may not be said to be a servant of God since he or she needs to grow in the Spirit first before he can be considered a servant of God. There are some Christians who are born again years ago yet they remain babes. This is not the way God plans them to be.

Servant Of Men: There are servants of men who have no other work but to please men. They preach the messages that please men even though the messages do not profit them eternally. These servants will do anything to please every member of his church. They are like politicians who count on the votes of the people to get them to the corridor of power. So they do everything - anything to get their approvals. Servants of men also count so much on men before they would prosper in their ministries. They rely on what men will give to them before they can work. Such servants are not really doing what God sent them but what people want them to do. The Bible says in Ephesians chapter 6: 5-6, *"Servants, be obedient to them that are your masters according to the flesh, with fear and trembling, in singleness of your heart, as unto Christ;*

"Not with eye service, as men pleasers; but as the servants of Christ, doing the will of God from the heart..."

Colossians 3:22, stresses, *"Servants, obey in all things your masters according to the flesh; not with eye service, as men pleasers; but in singleness of heart, fearing God."*

These passages indicate that there are people that are more of servants of men than servants of God.

I was in one Church one day when a Pastor said to the congregation, "I will do everything possible to please you in this Church." I wondered how this Pastor would please the people and preach the truth to them at the same time. There is no way a servant can please God and please man at the same time. Another negative thing about servants of men is that they are always closer to the rich people than other people. All these, however, are not rigid measure to know the servants of God or servants of men.

Servant Of Themselves: The book of Ezekiel 34:10 says: *"Thus saith the Lord GOD; Behold, I am against the shepherds; and I will require my flock at their hand, and cause them to cease from feeding the flock; neither shall the shepherds feed themselves any more; for I will deliver my flock from their mouth, that they may not be meat for them."*

From the above passage we can see that some servants use the congregation of the Lord to serve themselves. People may see them as servants of God but they are actually serving themselves, using and manipulating the people to accomplish their desires. This type of servants do not care about the eternity of other people but care so much about what they can get from them. All they are care about is themselves.

I remember how a man cared for his chicken so much that he never let anyone of them to be short of feeds. He was always ready to go hungry just to make sure that the chickens are well fed. Not that he loved the chicken but he had to feed them up so that when it is Christmas time, he would make enough money from the sales of each one of them. Servants of their flesh may care so much for the flocks solely because of their personal gain, not really because they care for their souls.

Servant Of The Devil: While God can still treat the three types of servants explained above as vessels of honour or dishonour that was indicated in 2 Timothy 2:20 respectively, He cannot use servants of the devil to teach or preach His word. God can use the vessels of honour or dishonour to bring about salvation and even miracles in the lives of people but that is not a proof that the servants will make heaven according to Matthew 7: 21-23. The reason God cannot use servants of the devil lies in the fact that they are possessed with anti-Christ spirits. If there is any sigh of wonders in the works of servants of the devil, it is demonic power. Jesus said in Matthew 7:15, **_"Beware of false prophets, which come to you in sheep's clothing, but inwardly they are ravening wolves."_**

The main purpose the devil sends his servants to pose as servants of God or to establish anti-Christ activities in or through various Churches or ministries is to deceive and devour souls of men, according to I Peter 5:8. They influence real believers to depart from faith through seducing spirits, heresies and lies, according to I Timothy 4:1-2. If there is any so-called blessing for these servants, it is not from God because He will not give His children's bread (blessings) to dogs (unbeliever) as pointed out in Matthew 15:26. Philippians 3:2 says, _"Beware of dogs, beware of evil workers, beware of the concision."_

Having enumerated the four kinds of servants, it is instructive to note that anybody can choose to be what he wants to be among them. It is a matter of choice. In 1 King18:21, the Bible says, **_"And Elijah came unto all the people, and said, How long halt ye between two opinions? if the LORD be God, follow him: but if Baal, then follow him. And the people answered him not a word."_** This passage indicates that God gives everybody the power to choose whom he or she wants to serve - God or the gods of this world that appear in different forms - money, lusts, entertainments, idolatry, ritualism, human worship and so many endless forms. Every one of us must choose whether we like it or not.

101

The eternal destination of each of the servants should be the most powerful consideration to become a servant of God. While a number servants of the devil are becoming servants of God by coming to the knowledge of Jesus Christ as I have seen and heard of so many cases, many servants of God through the compromise or disobedient to the word of God are becoming the servants of men or their flesh.

It is my prayer that before you complete this course, you would have become well established in the ministries the Lord has called you into.

VESSELS

Having studied about the various servants that are available all over the world, it is necessary to study the two types of vessels that are available for God's use.

In Romans 9:21-23, the Bible says, ***"Does not the potter have power over the clay, from the same lump to make one vessel for honour and another for dishonour? What if God, wanting to show His wrath and to make His power known, endured with much longsuffering the vessels of wrath prepared for destruction, and that He might make known the riches of His glory on the vessels of mercy, which He had prepared beforehand for glory..."*** From this passage and from the study of various servants, we can infer two types of vessels. One can be referred to as Vessel Of God or Vessel Of Honour while the other can be referred to as Borrowed Vessel or Vessel Of Dishonour. Let us study each of them.

Vessel Of God or Honour: When I was a civil servant in 1995, God told me to preach to my boss in the office. I found it very hard to obey Him because the boss loved me very much. He has done so much favours that I did not want to risk thwarting my relationship with him for whatever reason. By then, I was in the process of spiritual growth. So I did not understand the implication of disobeying God. Many of priorities were misplaced.

Few months later, this man was transferred to another district, where I never had the privilege to see him again. After another few months, I had a dream that I was sleeping in my room while I was actually sleeping, making the dream to appear so real. The boss entered and popped his eyes at me, pointing accusing finger at me and growling in a very deep voice, "you're a wicked man. When people see us together, they would think you love me but you never love me." I became so frightened in the dream that, when I woke, I was still gripped with horror. I knew the reason for the accusation but I did not know that the man was dying, if not dead at that time. I could not reach him to make amendment before I heard the news that he was dead. I decided to have a marathon fasting and prayers for days, asking for nothing from God but forgiveness of sins. When God spoke to me, it was a warning. He said, *"disobedience to My voice is a debt which someone has to pay for. Your disobedience has cost Me a soul. If you have obeyed me, the soul would have come to Me. Obedience to My voice is a blessing to My people, including the person that obeys Me. I am making you a vessel of honour. Do not disobey My voice again and I will use you to the fullness of your potentials."*

It is instructive to note the following characteristics in the vessels of honour, going by the word of God and my experience:

1. They hear the voice of God and obey Him to the last letter. (John 10:14-16)
2. They are made clean by the word of God (John 10:3).
3. They abide in Jesus Christ and bear good fruits (John 15:5).

To be prepared to be a vessel of honour takes process. The vessel often times need to pass through fire or wilderness experience so that they will understand that they should not live by bread alone but by every word of God (Deuteronomy 8:1-5). Because a lot of Christians who could be made into vessels of God are not willing to pass through this process, there are few labourers in the vineyard of God (Matthew 9:37). Since the harvest is much and the vessels are few, God has to use vessels of dishonour or borrow the vessels among the servants of themselves or other things.

Vessels Of Dishonour or Borrowed Vessels: Even though God would have preferred to use His own vessels, He is often forced to borrow vessels for His own use by the unavailability of His children. Take the case of my disobedience as an example. Do not be surprised that God uses some people that are not really His servants to do His work. God had been doing this right from the time Jesus was on earth. Jesus sees the Pharisees and the Sadducees as borrows vessels. So He told the disciples that they should do as they say but not as they do (Matthew 23:1-7).

A preacher delivered a powerful sermon on the radio one day. A Pastor living in that area felt the need to meet the preacher and congratulate him for the message. On getting to the premises of the radio station, he asked about the preacher. The staff of the radio station pointed at him, coming out of the studio with two shamelessly dressed ladies supporting him to his car. The Pastor was disappointed but he does not need to for the mere fact that the preacher was a borrowed vessel.

Some borrowed vessels may be used by God for signs and wonders but, going by the passage in Matthew 7:21-23, they will be cast away on the day of judgment. Many people concluded that because God uses them, they belong to Him. Note that spiritual gifts cannot improvise for salvation. There are so many spiritually gifted Christians that will end up in hell. In Matthew 7:21-23, Jesus said, *"Not every one that saith unto me, Lord, Lord, shall enter into the kingdom of heaven; but he that doeth the will of my Father which is in heaven. Many will say to me in that day, Lord, Lord, have we not prophesied in thy name? and in thy name have cast out devils? and in thy name done many wonderful works? And then will I profess unto them, I never knew you: depart from me, ye that work iniquity."*

Some people who went through Near Death Experience as in my case are given the chance to see what is going on in heaven. Some of them explained that there many mansions in heaven as a result of some of their good works of people but the owners are in hell because of the sins in their lives.

Knowing vessels of honour and dishonour is simple enough. All you need to do is to observe their fruits. Jesus said in Matthew 7:16 that you will know them by their fruits.

WHAT MINISTRY IS ALL ABOUT

There are so many misconceptions about ministry. Many people think ministry implies having a Church or an independent work of the Lord. Ministry as a matter of fact is doing things in the name of the Lord. Colossians 3:16-17, the Bible says, *"Let the word of Christ dwell in you richly in all wisdom; teaching and admonishing one another in Psalms and hymns and spiritual songs, singing with grace in your hearts to the Lord. And whatsoever you do in word or deed, do all in the name of the Lord Jesus, giving thanks to God and the Father by him."* From this passage we can say ministry is ministering to the Lord, to fellow believers and to the world with what God has given us in terms of gifts, talents and substances. In the book of Ephesians 2:10, the Bible says, *"For we are his workmanship, created in Christ Jesus unto good works, which God hath before ordained that we should walk in them."*

There are ministries that are general to all Christians and there are some that are peculiar to callings. In either ways, the works of the ministries which the Lord had committed into hands of believers are done in words, deeds and spirit. Anything done in the flesh is enmity with God. Romans 8:7-8 the Bible says, *"Because the carnal mind is enmity against God: for it is not subject to the law of God, neither indeed can be. So then they that are in the flesh cannot please God."*

I know of some Christians who lost their lives because they are involved in the kind of ministries that are peculiar to the callings of others. They died of ignorance. God trains and equips people before they are involved in certain ministries, especially specific ones. Just as there are different forces like the soldiers, navy and air forces that are trained to function very effectively in their respective fields, soldiers of Christ are also trained by God to perform effectively in the different areas of their callings.

I would like to cite myself as an example. I have been a writer since I was a teenager. I have read so many books that aid me in creative writings. Most of these books had negative influence in my life and writings before I gave my life to Christ. When I gave my life to Christ, I expected God to immediately start using me to write evangelical materials. I was shocked when He said He could not use me then. My head, according to Him, was full of debris which I had acquired as knowledge from the books I have read. My head needs purification with the word of God. So for years, He took me through His Words, using at times Christian literatures to establish me firmly. It was about 12 years after I got converted that God made a way for me to be a columnist in 1993 in Nigerian Tribune, one of the few national newspapers at that time.

I also know some people who are not making impact in their ministries because they are not doing what the Lord sent them to do. There are, however, certain ministries that are for all Christians, irrespective of the time they are converted. No matter the specific ministry God gives to a person, he or she must be involved in the general ministries.

GENERAL MINISTRIES

The ministries that are given to all Christians are: (A) Ministry To The Lord (B) Ministry To The family (C) Ministries In The Church (D) Ministries Of Help (E) Ministries To The World.

Ministry To The Lord: Salvation is a very personal issue that involves a deep relationship between God and the believer. The intimate relationship brings about communion with the Lord through prayers, quiet time, adoration, praise and worship to Him. The relationship through this communion is the foundation of other ministries. No matter how great the work a Christian is doing for the Lord, this communion must not be neglected or compromised. It is through the relationship of a Christian with God that he or she taps into His strength and gets directions and instructions. He also gets to know more about God and what He has for him or her and others through this relationship and communion. If a Christian does not hear from God or know about Him and His ways, what will he teach other people?

To really minister unto the Lord, a Christian must always adore, praise and worship God. Sometimes all a person needs in a particular situation is just to praise and worship God as in the story Israelites and the wall of Jericho. In Joshua 6:20, the Bible says. *"So the people shouted when the priests blew with the trumpets: and it came to pass, when the people heard the sound of the trumpet, and the people shouted with a great shout, that the wall (of Jericho) fell down flat, so that the people went up into the city, every man straight before him, and they took the city."*

If this area is given a serious attention, there is no way the Christian will lose his bearing or fail in his ministries or other areas of his life. In John 15:4, Jesus said, *"Abide in me, and I in you. As the branch cannot bear fruit of itself, except it abide in the vine; no more can ye, except ye abide in me."* In other words, the relationship of every believer matters in everything he or she does in life.

Ministry To The Family: The ministry of every Christian, especially married people begins from home. A man and woman who does not marry according to the will of God usually encounter unnecessary problems in their marriages and other ministries either in the Church and or in other places. It is ideal to treat how a Christian can get the knowledge of the will of God in area of marriage, calling, career and other things.

Knowledge Of The Will Of God: The followings are ways God reveal His will to His people:

1. So many times God reveals His will to His children through dreams or still small voice or vision. In Luke 1: 11-15, we see how God revealed Himself and His will to Zechariah through vision. In Genesis 37: 5-9, we also see how God revealed His will and plan to Joseph through dreams.
2. The Bible says in Psalms 37:31, *"The law of his God in his heart; none of his steps shall slide."* This means that through His word, God can speak and lead to us. No matter which way a person gets to know the will of God, the will or voice of God will never contradict His

word. I remember a man who gambled about the will of God in area of marriage. He told God that the first sister that came to the Church one Sunday would be assumed as the person He had provided for him as his wife. When the first sister came to the church, she turned out to be the Pastor's wife.

3. First Thessalonians 5:20 says, *"Despise not prophesying."* In other words, the will or the mind of God can be known through prophesy. Prophesy can come through the words of a preacher or other person.

4. Some people may not have the gift of discernment or revelations or visions. So God at times use circumstances to reveal His will to such people like in the case of Abraham's servant who was told to get a wife for Isaac as recorded in Genesis 24:1-21.

Again, there must confirmation of the will of God to the person or another person. This makes the person sure he is doing the will of God. Besides, the enemy of our souls can go to the extent of using any or all of the above to divert children of God from His will without even contradicting the word of God. He is as smart as that. To illustrate this, I would love to share the testimony of a sister with you.

A sister I would call Victoria (not her real name) dreamt that she was married to John (not real name). Victoria went to tell her pastor what she dreamt. The pastor told her to go and pray as he took up the matter. The pastor called John and asked him if God has spoken to him about the sister he would marry. John had not taken time to pray about that. So he was also told to go and pray. When he prayed, he dreamt that he was married to another sister called Mary (not her real name). The pastor called Mary and asked the question he asked John. God has already revealed it Mary that she was going to marry John. Today Mary and John are happily married, doing very great in their pastoral and outreach ministries. All these did not take place within a short time. If the devil have succeeded in manipulating the plan of God for this couple, their ministries would have become history even before they start.

God is always willing to speak through one way or the other to any of His children who really wants to know and follow his will.

Having treated ways of knowing the will of God, it is also good to treat why God will never speak or reveal His mind to some Christians no matter how much they pray.

Hindrances In Knowing The Will Of God: The followings are things that hinder a Christian from knowing the will of God.

Un-repented Sin: This can make God not to hear a Christian. In

Isaiah 59: 1-2, the Bible says, *"behold the Lord's hand is not shortened, that it cannot save, neither his ear heavy that it cannot hear: But your iniquities have separated between you and your God, and y our sins have hid his face from you, that he will not hear."*

Some Christians commit sins which they feel God will overlook without knowing that they are moving gradually away from the reach of God to where He will neither hear nor speak to them. If a Christian that commits sin claim to hear from God, the chances are that he hears the voice of his flesh or that of the devil or the combination of the two.

Disobedience: The Bible says in I Samuel 15:23, *"For rebellion is as the sin of witchcraft, and stubbornness is an iniquity ad idolatry, because thou has rejected the word of the Lord, he hath rejected thee from being king."*

When God specifically instructs a Christian to do a thing and he refuses to do it, God may stop speaking to him.

A woman asked God to do something about her unfulfilled life in the civil service. God told her to resign her appointment with the Government and take up petty trading. She found it hard to believe that it was an instruction from God. So she refused to resign her appointment with the government. God stopped speaking to her. She went to complain to her Pastor about not hearing from God again. God told the Pastor that he will not speak to her until she did what He had instructed her to do. The Pastor told her what God said. She immediately went to do what God wanted. This woman later became so successful in the business that she gives so much into the work of God.

Complaint Or Ungratefulness: in 1 Thessalonians 5:18, the Bible says, *"In every thing give thanks: for this is the will of God in Christ Jesus concerning you."* One of the things God hates is complaint. When Christian complains about their conditions instead of thanking God for the blessing of life and the life in Christ, they are telling God He is not caring. God will not only be hurt but also feel offended. This can bring lots of problems into the life of the Christian as in the case of the people of Israel who never got to the promised land in Numbers chapters 14 to 16. Complaints hinder prayers and prevents God from hearing anybody that complaints.

Having treated the few ways to know the will of God and hindrances in knowing the will, it must be noted that the ministry to the family is the Primary Ministry of a Christian. If he fails in it, he is likely going to fail in others. I related a story about a deaconess in the resource materials titled: Christian Orientation Course Book. The deaconess' husband went to complain to the pastor of her Church, saying that if his wife could be made the deaconess with her type of attitude, then he was qualified to be the General Overseer of all the branches of the Church even though he did not claim to be a righteous man like his wife. For this reason, let us now study the basic ministry to the family.

The Basic Ministry To The Family: The Bible says in I Timothy 5: 8, *"But if any provide not for his own, and especially for those of his own house, he hath denied the faith, and is worse than an infidel."*

The provisions to the family are in two ways which are physical and spiritual.

Physical Provision: God made the husband the head and the wife must be subjected to him according to Ephesians 5:22-24. The passage says, *"Wives, submit yourselves unto your own husbands, as unto the Lord. For the husband is the head of the wife, even as Christ is the head of the church: and he is the Saviour of the body. Therefore as the church is subject unto Christ, so let the wives be to their own husbands in every thing."*

One can see the need for a Christian to marry according to the prefect will of God. If a Christian sister marries an unbeliever, she would be giving the spiritual authority over her body to the wrong person. It would be a different case, however, if she had married before she became born-again. If that case, the message in I Corinthians 7:10-16 will apply to the Christian whether a man or woman. The passage says, *"And unto the married I command, yet not I, but the Lord, Let not the wife depart from her husband: But and if she depart, let her remain unmarried, or be reconciled to her husband: and let not the husband put away his wife. But to the rest speak I, not the Lord: If any brother hath a wife that believeth not, and she be pleased to dwell with him, let him not put her away.*

"And the woman which hath a husband that believeth not, and if he be pleased to dwell with her, let her not leave him.

"For the unbelieving husband is sanctified by the wife, and the unbelieving wife is sanctified by the husband: else were your children unclean; but now are they holy.

"But if the unbelieving depart, let him depart. A brother or a sister is not under bondage in such cases: but God hath called us to peace. For what knowest thou, O wife, whether thou shalt save thy husband? or how knowest thou, O man, whether thou shalt save thy wife?"

109

While the wife must submit herself to her husband, he in return must love her according to the instructions in Ephesians 5:25-31 which says, *"Husbands, love your wives, even as Christ also loved the church, and gave himself for it;*

"That he might sanctify and cleanse it with the washing of water by the word,

"That he might present it to himself a glorious church, not having spot, or wrinkle, or any such thing; but that it should be holy and without blemish.

"So ought men to love their wives as their own bodies. He that loveth his wife loveth himself.

"For no man ever yet hated his own flesh; but nourisheth and cherisheth it, even as the Lord the church: For we are members of his body, of his flesh, and of his bones.

"For this cause shall a man leave his father and mother, and shall be joined unto his wife, and they two shall be one flesh."

As Jesus loves and provides for the Church, the husband must love and provide for his family, including the children. There must be mutual agreement between the two before any of them can do anything that is of mutual interest.

According to what Jesus said in Matthew 19:3-11, divorce is not an option for Christians. In Verse 3-9; the Bible says, *"The Pharisees also came unto him (Jesus), tempting him, and saying unto him, Is it lawful for a man to put away his wife for every cause?*

"And he answered and said unto them, Have ye not read, that he which made them at the beginning made them male and female.

"And said, For this cause shall a man leave father and mother, and shall cleave to his wife: and they twain shall be one flesh?

"Wherefore they are no more twain, but one flesh. What therefore God hath joined together, let not man put asunder.

"They say unto him, Why did Moses then command to give a writing of divorcement, and to put her away?

"He saith unto them, Moses because of the hardness of your hearts suffered you to put away your wives: but from the beginning it was not so.

"And I say unto you, Whosoever shall put away his wife, except it be for fornication, and shall marry another, committeth adultery: and whoso marrieth her which is put away doth commit adultery."

Since it is impossible to divide the body of a person without taking his life, it is not possible also to divide a couple that are joined together by God without affecting their eternal lives. The devil aims at destroying eternal lives. Hence, he threatens marriages with every available weapon or tool. He knows that if he breaks or divides couples, he would be dividing the entire family, including their children's children.

Couples must understand that marriage is a product of God. To know how to operate this product, the couple must consult the manual. As it is normal for users to have problems with products, they can fix them by consulting the manufacturers. Likewise, if couples have problems with their marriages, destroying them is not an option, especially when they are conscious of the fact that they cannot marry again except if their spouses die. All they need to do is to consult the Manufacturer - God if they have problems with the product - the marriage. The couples have responsibilities on their parts to make their marriages work the way God wants them to work, according to the manual of the product called the Bible. The Bible says in John 10:10 that the devil has the missions to steal, to kill and to destroy. Hence he wants to steal the joy of their marriages, kill couples spiritually and destroy their eternal lives in hell. It is up to them to stay married for life, making the Bible the guiding principles of their marriages.

Parents must provide for all the needs of their children until they are old enough to be on their own. They must always prove it to their children that they love them by showing love to each other. Couples must see their marriages as lasting legacies that provide role models to the children and their children's children. They must also train them in the way they should go according to Proverb 22:6. The wife must build her house by meeting the emotional needs of her husband and children. She must always be there to comfort and encourage each member of her family. In Proverb 14:1 the Bible says, *"Every wise woman buildeth her house: but the foolish plucketh it down with her hands."* In other words, she must be ready to sacrifice many things to save her marriage. There are always strange women whom the devil have set up to take her husband from her. There are negative influences, ungodly films and programs on the television which the devil can use to lure the children away from the right way. Real mother must guard against all acts that can have negative influence on them through prayer and through all she can to ensure that the fear of God reigns in her family.

In conclusion to the physical provisions, couples must understand that the marriage is not all about individual interests but about God, the spouse comes second, the children come next and other things come next. The individual interests come last. If this order of priority is misplaced, the wife or the husband would always clamour for his or her rights. If this order is follow, the husband would always put the interests of his wife ahead of his. The same is also applicable to the wife. The misplacement of priorities always brings about selflessness, lack of considerations for others and lack of mutual care and understanding, which can lead to emotional detachments. There would be selfishness, sel-frighteousness or complaints like, "you always hurt my feelings," "you never put me into considerations," "It's my money we've been spending together" and a host of others like that. Any accusation always brings about counter accusation. Any consideration always brings about consideration from the other person. It is like if you show your spouse the saint inside you, he or she will naturally show you his or her saint. If you show him or her your beast, all you'll see is his or her own beast too.

Spiritual Provision: This has to do with the family alter. There should be a family altar every morning and evening or at least once in a day. The family is a mini Church or an arm of the Church of God where only family members gather, worship God, praise Him, share His word and make their daily requests to Him. Some families have a small chapel in their houses. This may not be necessary for families that cannot afford to build any. Actually, the Church is not a building. It is a congregation of the people that makes the Church. It is easy to know through the traits exhibited by the children if a family congregates everyday to worship God.

Some years ago, my daughter went to spend her holiday with a family in a city. When I asked her how she spent her holidays, her first and only complaint was that the family do not congregate to pray everyday as she was used to. For that reason, she said she would like to spend her next holiday elsewhere.

If families actually make Jesus their head, then there is need to talk to Him everyday.

Having touched some basic things in the ministry to the family, we can now talk on the ministry in the Church.

BASIC MINISTRIES IN THE CHURCH

Even if a Christian is called into a specific ministry outside the church, he needs be identified with a local Church or what I called Home Church. He or she needs to first start the specific ministry among the congregation of the people of God - be it healing, teaching, deliverance, music, drama or whatever. I began my publication, drama and teaching ministry right in the Church. The Church, according to I Corinthians 12:14-30, is a Body of Christ which is made up of members. The members of the Body are the Christians that play many roles within and outside the Church. Verse 21 says, "*And the eye cannot say unto the hand, I have no need of thee; nor again the head to the feet, I have no need of you.*" Since, according to the passage, it is now established that all Christians need one another to be effective in their ministries in the Church or outside, it follows therefore that every Christian needs to be involved in one ministry or the other in the Church.

I want to distinguish general ministries from specific ones in the passage above. In specific ministries which we are going to discuss later, Church leaders like the Pastors, Evangelists, etc are specifically called and ordained by God to lead the Church or ministries while the general ministries are what every Christian must be involved in, using the gifts God has given to each Christian. Please note that just because a person is gifted in miracle or healing does not mean that he can lead a Church or ministry. In fact, before God can call anyone to lead any ministry which involves the births and sustenance of eternal lives, he must have been trained by God. It is a pity that a lot of Christians who are supposed to be followers have assumed the positions of leadership in some Churches and ministries because they are so gifted. When such person becomes a leader, the ministry becomes man or self made. Such ministries become vulnerable to the attack of enemies. If man would not commit the lives of the armies into the hands of untrained captains to lead, how can anyone expect God to commit eternal lives of His people into the hands of ministers that lack training? It must thus be understood that specific ministries is for people that are specifically and specially ordained and called by God into the specific ministries.

Intercessory Ministry: This is the ministry every Church must be involved in because every believer is called to talk with God and intercede for others, himself and the world. In Ephesians 6:18, the Bible says, "*Praying always with all prayer and supplication in the Spirit, and watching thereunto with all perseverance and supplication for all saints.*"

We can see in this passage that Christians are to pray for other people. In so doing we are caring for one another.

I related the story of an elder woman who was an usher in a church in one of the course books. The Church always witnessed outstanding

113

miracles until the elderly woman died. The Pastor of the church was worried that the Church no longer witness miracles since the death of the woman. So he sought the Lord in prayer. God told him that it was the elderly woman exercising her gift in miracles, praying and often times fasting so that the people in the Church would experience outstanding miracles. Since the woman is gone, there was no one to stand in the gap for the miracles.

Intercessory ministries include the followings:

i. Communing or talking with God like a son talking to his Father as in the case of Habakkuk 3: 1-2. God delights in hearing and talking with His children.

ii. Worshiping God, singing spiritual songs (Ephesians 5:19).

iii. Asking God to do things with right motives (James 4:2-3)

All Christians must be involved in intercessory ministries, especially at this time when the devil is fighting the last battle with everybody, doing all he can to get people to hell. They need to pray for the harvest of souls of men because their spiritual lives depend on them. Any Christian is who not involved in intercessory ministries may dry up and may eventually backslide even if others are praying for him.

Ministry Of Help: The ministry of help can come in three ways but the greatest challenge of this ministry which is also the greatest problem in the Body Of Christ is disunity. Because of this problem, most do not want to render help in any kind unless they know something is coming out of it. Besides, they render help to those they are familiar with.

The ministry of help is so important in Christianity that without it, other ministries cannot be effective. Through ministry of help, Christians show love, trust and diligence in their faith. These are the bedrock of sound Christian faith. If Christians preach love, they must demonstrate it through love, giving and care.

A missionary picked a girl who has lost both parents during a civil war in the street in one country. She did all she could do to help the girl, including taking her into a Christian orphanage centre. The girl said, 'I know you are doing this so that you can get to heaven.' The missionary was hurt but she never blamed her because the girl's life was characterized with hatred for everybody. This was one of the results of the civil war in the country. When the missionary was about to leave for another place, she told the girl to kiss her goodbye. It was then the girl saw genuine love. She burst out crying, saying, 'please, don't leave me alone!'

In James 4:17 the Bible says, ***"Therefore to him that knoweth to*** *do good and doeth it not, to him it is a sin."* In other words, if the ministry of help which is doing good to others is not carried out by a Christian he is actually committing a sin. It is therefore a little wonder the prayer of many Christians are not answered. In Psalms 66:18, we read, *"If I regard iniquity in my heart, the Lord will not hear me."*

Not getting involved in ministry of help can result into iniquity because everything a Christian has, including his potentials and substance, actually belongs to God and must be used to the glory of the Lord.

The three ways which Christians must be involved in ministry of help are as follows:

Deeds: In James 2:17, the Bible says, *"Even so faith, if it hath not works, is dead, being alone."* This passage indicates that the work of a Christian in any ministry must reflect his faith. In Colossians 3:17, the Bible says, *"And whatsoever ye do in word or deed, do all in the name of the Lord Jesus, giving thanks to God and the Father by him."*

Deeds as general ministries of all Christians are carried out by rendering services that would bless the people whether they are believers or not; as long as the services are rendered in the name of the Lord Jesus. The services may be in form of works in the Church, visiting and praying for the elderly people in their homes, ministering to the sick in the hospitals, prisoners in prisons, following up new converts, teaching people the word of God everywhere etc. The services must be in the name of the Lord, not necessarily to make money but to bless souls. Deeds of all Christians matter a lot in every ministry to the family, to the Church and also to the world.

Counseling: In Psalms 33: 11, the Bible says, *"The counsel of the LORD standeth for ever, the thoughts of his heart to all generations."*

The above passage indicates that the Lord has a counsel. The only people He can use to counsel every category of people are the Christians. Therefore every Christian must always influence people positively with the counsel of the Lord. Unknown to many Christian, a lot of people are fed up with their lives, waiting for someone to give them hope. When Christians who have solution to their problems do not go to them with the counsel of the Lord, the people sometimes take their own lives or turn to other things that promise solutions. The solutions to all problems and pains that people go through can be made available through the counsel of the Lord. Thus Christians must always seek to give the counsel of the Lord even if the people feel they do not need it.

A sister was sitting down outside a house one day, reading Bible when the Holy Spirit told her to counsel a man that was carrying a table into his room. She did not yield, thinking that she would be regarded as a nuisance or an intruder into someone else's privacy. The man got out of the house to go and take a chair after putting the table inside. Still, this sister did not yield to the leading of the Lord. Finally the man got a rope, entered his room; put the chair on the table; fixed the rope on a ceiling fan and hanged himself. It was when the man was found dead that this sister realized that she has a soul to account for in heaven. She cried and lamented for many days.

Christians must not feel like a nuisance or intruder when they seek the opportunity to counsel others about their lives, business, marriages and other things. The book of Ezekiel 33:7-10 says, *"So thou, O son of man, I have set thee a watchman unto the house of Israel; therefore thou shalt hear the word at my mouth, and warn them from me.*

"When I say unto the wicked, O wicked man, thou shalt surely die; if thou dost not speak to warn the wicked from his way, that wicked man shall die in his iniquity; but his blood will I require at thine hand.

"Nevertheless, if thou warn the wicked of his way to turn from it; if he does not turn from his way, he shall die in his iniquity; but thou hast delivered thy soul.

"Therefore, O thou son of man, speak unto the house of Israel; Thus ye speak, saying, If our transgressions and our sins be upon us, and we pine away them, how should we then live?"

This passage obviously makes all Christians watchmen over the souls of others.

Giving: All Christians must learn how to give because it is a way to prove that what they have actually belong to God. In second Corinthians 9:6-8, the Bible says; *"But this I say, He which soweth sparingly shall reap also sparingly; and he which soweth bountifully shall reap also bountifully.*

"Every man according as he purposeth in his heart, so let him give; not grudgingly, or of necessity: for God loveth a cheerful giver.

"And God is able to make all grace abound toward you; that ye, always having all sufficiency in all things, may abound to every good work."

Giving is a good work, according to that passage. It is also an attribute of God because He first gave us the very best of Himself by giving us Jesus to die for us. God would rather readily use the gifts and potentials of His children to either bless others or for His works than to borrow vessels for the same use. Christians must not give because they want God to bless them even though He definitely will. But their giving must be as they purpose in their hearts, especially when they see the need. Christians who want the work of the Lord to progress must give, not until they are forced. I would like to use the story of a teenager in one of my books to illustrate how giving won a whole family to Christ through giving.

The teenage boy went to preach to a family who, unknown to him, were going through hard time. The father was as hungry as his wife and children. The man glared at the boy when he said he has come to preach to the family. He threatened to beat the boy up if he did to get out of his house. Sensing their problem, the boy went to get some food items from his parents. He went back to the family and gave it to the man. He was given an audience immediately. The family became Christians afterwards.

Contrary to what many people think, every Christian has something to give. No one in the world is born empty. The followings are the ways Christians can give to the Lord.

(1) By paying their tithes and offerings regularly in the house of the Lord (Malachi 3:8-12).

(2) By giving to those who are in need. Anybody that gives to needy people, especially fellow Christians is actually giving to the Lord according to (Matthew 25: 35-46).

(3) Christians can actually give to God by using their talents to the glory of the Lord (Matthew 25:14-30). Talents do not mean only natural abilities or spiritual gifts of Christians but can also mean their time, money, skills and potentials.

It is when a Christian has used what God has given him that He can bless him and give him more talents or skills. Any Christian who feels too big to spend his time doing little work like cleaning the house of the God is actually too little to do other work, going by my experience.

MINISTRIES TO THE WORLD

In Mark 16:15-17, the Bible says, And he said unto them, *"Go ye into all the world, and preach the gospel to every creature.*

"He that believeth and is baptized shall be saved; but he that believeth not shall be damned.

"And these signs shall follow them that believe; In my name shall they cast out devils; they shall speak with new tongues."

117

The work of soul winning is a very vital and urgent ministry of all Christians. God relies on His children to win souls for Him. He could have given the assignment to angels who would be much more effective but He chooses to give His people the privilege so that they can get the reward in heaven.

Preaching the word of God to sinners is important to them and to God. The word that is preached to sinners is what God will use to either save them from condemnation or to condemn them on the Day of Judgment. It is when a sinner is saved that he can enjoy the privileges that go along with salvation on earth. The greatest miracle on earth is salvation. Every other miracle will end on earth but salvation is of eternal value. That is the reason there is joy in heaven when a soul is saved. Luke 15:7

The simplest forms of evangelism that require nothing but the soul winner and the person(s) that is to be won for Christ are (1) Personal Evangelism (2) Lifestyle Evangelism.

Personal Evangelism: This is a direct contact with the person to be converted. Through sharing testimony with the person alone is enough to persuade him to come to the knowledge of Christ. By talking with the person, the soul winner has the privilege of leading him directly to Christ without using tools that are used in mass evangelism.

Lifestyle Evangelism: This has to do with the way of life of the soul winner. Hence, his life does more of the preaching than mere words. In 2 Corinthians 3:2-3, the Bible says, *"You are our epistle written in our hearts, known and read by all men."* There are so many cases of people giving their lives to Christ as a result of studying the lives of some Christians.

Having studied, the basic ministries of all Christians, you are better equipped to carry out the functions that are expected of you in your environment with what God has given you so far. Begin right now with what you have and from where you are and then expect God to bless you in return.

EVANGELISM METHODOLOGY

(BOOK SIX)

118

INTRODUCTION

Permit me to introduce this subject with the testimony of how I got converted. I am sure there is a lesson to learn.

It was in the year 1992, one midnight, the time everybody has gone to sleep when the incident that would transform my life took place. Before then a Christian sister who lived in another town was interceding on my behalf. Her concern for my salvation made her to pray for me through out the particular night I had the encounter with the Lord.

As I was sleeping, I suddenly felt my spirit leaving my body into another realm. It was a place I was to be judged according to my ways. What I saw there was quite unexpected. There were many people who had preached to me at one time or the other, waiting to testify against me. Each one of them gave the day and time he or she preached to me but I never yielded. After everyone had testified against me, I told myself that I was doomed. Then I heard the voice of Jesus saying, "I'm giving you the last chance to mend your ways and follow me."

My spirit came back into my body and, of course, I became a new person that day.

Now evangelism is not just preaching the word of God to people so that they can be converted but for God to have something in His record that the word was preached to them. That is why this subject is very crucial to every believer, including the newly converted Christians. Before talking about evangelism, let us first revisit the issue the three persons in one person as treated in Deliverance In General so as to refresh or further understand the principle of Total Person.

TOTAL PERSON

Being a total person simply means a complete person. What makes a person complete is not whether he or she can produce or not or whether he is normal person or not.

The complete person God created comprises of The Body (physical being), The Spirit (the spiritual being) and The Soul (the emotional being). That is to say man is a tripartite being. That means he exists in three parts. The three parts which makes a person complete is also explained with the diagram below, based on 1Thessalonians 5:23, which says, *"And the very God of peace sanctify you wholly; and I pray God your whole spirit and soul and body be preserved blameless unto the coming of our Lord Jesus Christ."*

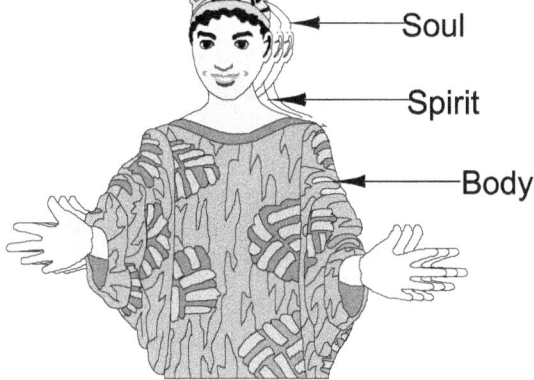

THE BODY (PHYSICAL BEING): This is the part of human being that can be seen with the eyes or through the use of any equipment like X-ray machines. This part had been studied by man. Hence experts like doctors know how each part of the body structure functions. When there is defect, man knows how to correct it with the use of drugs or other things. When the body wears out, however, the spirit and soul would have to leave the body. That means the person is dead. Some bodies last long and some do not either as a result of sickness, spiritual or emotional problems. In any case, we live longer than one another. Thus human bodies are the visible and mortal clothing that house the other two parts of human beings. Our bodies, therefore, need to be taken care of like properties because they house our souls and spirits. It is erroneous belief that when a person dies, he or she reincarnates. The Bible says in Hebrew 9:27 that it is appointed unto man once to die, but after this the judgment. This place makes it clear that once our bodies wear out and go back to the dust, the soul and the spirit do not stay in this world. We have more than enough evidences that prove this, including the testimonies of people that die and came back to life.

THE SPIRIT (SPIRITUAL BEING): This is the invisible part of a person. The Bible says in Genesis 2:7, *"And the LORD God formed man of the dust of the ground, and breathed into his nostrils the breath of life; and man became a living soul."* From this passage, it is clear that the breathe of God forms the (physical) life of man. Since God is a Spirit, according John 2:24, His breathe is also a Spirit. Because man needs this Spirit before he can live as a living soul in this world, he is given this Spirit (the breath of God), which become The Spirit of man.

121

Of course, this Spirit or breathe of God would still go back to the owner - God.

From the above explanations, we can see that The Spirit of man connects his soul and the body together. Once this breathe of God in man leaves, his life on earth ceased to exist. In other words, his body which goes back to the dust is separated from his soul.

The Spirit of man makes it possible for him to operate in the spirit realm. Irrespective of anyone's belief, there is a spirit realm from where what would happen in the physical realm is sometimes designed. That is why it is possible for a person to dream of what would happen before it actually happens. He gets this information through The Spirit of man which is also known as Spirit Man. It is only through the Spirit of man that man can know God. The Bible says in Gospel according to Saint John 4:24, *"God is a Spirit: and they that worship him must worship him in spirit and in truth."*

The reason many do not know God despite the works of His hands is that their spirits are inactive or dead. However, it can be made active or alive by influencing by preaching and teaching the person the Word of God, using the gateways in the body to the spirit and soul. The gateways are the human sense of perceptions like the eyes, ears, nose, mouth and the flesh. Whatever passes through these gateways has a way of influencing all the three parts of man. If what he takes is Godly, it would make him Godly. If it is demonic, of course, it will make him demonic. This influence is what affects his belief and his belief would determines the eternal destination of the soul when he dies physically.

There are lots of things going on in the spirit realm because the Supreme Being - God is a Spirit and the enemy of man - the devil is also a spirit. Angels and demons are also spirits. Two out of three parts of man - The Spirit and The Soul are also spirits. God who creates man wants him to be reconciled to Him through Jesus Christ after the fall of man (Hebrew 9:14-17). The devil also struggles to influence man through the effective use of things he can perceive with his human senses, trying all he can to control him through unclean and invisible spirits called demons.

The truth about the spirit realm is that God lives in the bodies of true Christians through Holy Spirit. The devil through demons also lives and controls the bodies of so many people. In other words, some people are under God's control while some are not. Some may be deceived that they are on their own but no one is independent of either of the control of God or the devil. Please, study the course book titled:

Deliverance In General, which is also in Christian Education Series.

THE SOUL (EMOTIONAL BEING): The soul is responsible for the emotional or mental well being of a person. Whatever goes wrong or right with the spirit affects the soul. So the spirit needs to be fed with right thing the gateways in human body. The Bible says in Ezekiel 18:20, *"The soul that sins, it shall die. The son shall not bear the iniquity of the father, neither shall the father bear the iniquity of the son: the righteousness of the righteous shall be upon him, and the wickedness of the wicked shall be upon him."*

The death of a soul is different from the physical or spiritual death. The meaning of the death of a soul is found in Revelation 21:8 which says, *"But the fearful, and unbelieving, and the abominable, and murderers, and whoremonger, and sorcerers, and idolaters, and all liars, shall have their part in the lake which burns with fire and brimstone: which is the second death..."*

BUILDING THE TOTAL PERSON

Having studied what we need to know in the total person, let us study how the total person can be built. Please, note that the three parts of a person are very essential. They are so dependent on each other that none can be left out. For instance, you may not be able to successfully pass any message to a sick or emotionally depressed or spiritually tormented person. There are so many spiritually related cases being treated in the hospital or in other places.

There are certain methods that can be applied to develop all the three parts. Let us discuss that first.

TEACHING METHOD: Teaching method in this regard does not imply teaching methodology but teaching the person orally or through the use of materials like books, visual aids and other things. When you teach a person a subject, he or she believes it, especially if he or she is young. Researches I conducted while gathering information I use in my books titled "Foundation Bible Club Story Book", which are used as missionary tools to equip young minds, reveals that at tender age, children believe virtually everything. They believe that once the adults say it is so, then it must be so. They have no intellectual ability to question what they are taught unless they are being faced with facts that conflict it. At that age, they are still gathering information about life and looking for ways to approach it. Teaching method which can be formal or informal is often done orally or in written form.

What a person teaches a person goes a long way to affect a generation. If everybody is conscious of what he or she teaches others, a whole society can be repaired no matter the state of the society.

CONDUCT METHOD: A person is built through conduct of other people. Conduct in this regards can be described as coherent or set of acts that are seen or viewed as impressive or influential by others. Conduct may be seen in real life or fake life as people watch it on films or TV. Unknown to many people, what we see with our eyes either on TV or in places makes lasting impressions in on our minds.

Conduct feeds the Spirit Man with information through the gateways in the body. This explains the reason the media is so powerful. Many people develop negative or positive attitudes because they pick wrong or right persons as role models or heroes either in real life or on TV or other places. At times, I marveled at how people can be so gullible and easily fooled by what they watch on tv though no one needs to be surprised. The fact is that conduct which is addressed to the eyes makes it difficult for people to distinguish truths from lies, facts from fictions, reality and opinions. Some people get wrong information through fake life on the screen and begin to act on it. I have witnessed an occasion where a star was almost stoned to death in the street because she acted as a wicked woman in a Nigerian movie.

Information that is stored in the spirit of a person through conduct is often times difficult to delete. Hence, it is essential to be mindful of what you watch or what you allow your children to see anywhere.

ENTERTAINMENT METHOD: This is a way of passing messages in form of entertainment like music, movies, story books etc. What most people do not realize about this method is that it is the most effective method of passing messages whether negative or positive. So many countries are being influenced or brainwashed through movies and music. Please, study the results of my research works on how humanity is often times brainwashed in my book titled: The Insanity Of Humanity.

The world is easily deceived through entertainments that are usually packaged to look real. A boy in Nigeria shot his friend dead with his father's gun while trying to imitate his hero in a drama.

The messages in most songs, movies and media today are filled with subliminal messages that are intended to either corrupt the Spirit Man or lead the audience into the worship of demons.

INFORMATION AND EDUCATION METHOD: This method is a way of educating people in schools and sharing facts that are often backed with proofs like pictures and items. A typical example of this is found in documentary programs or videos like the testimony of a man that died and was preserved in the mortuary, coming back to life after four days. The film is titled "Raised from the Dead." Often times, information method is required to convince people of so many things, including spiritual things.

The above are the broad method that can be used to build or develop the three parts of a person. Having explained the three parts of man, we can now study evangelism.

WHAT IS EVANGELISM?

Evangelism is simply presentation of the word of God to people so that they may accept Jesus Christ as their Lord and Saviour, using the power of the Holy Spirit as recorded in Acts 1:8. It is also an act of preaching and warning people of eternal destruction. God says in Ezekiel 33:2-4, *"Son of man, speak to the children of your people, and say unto them, When I bring the sword upon a land, if the people of the land take a man from their territory, and set him for their watchman: When he sees the sword come upon the land, he blows the trumpet, and warns the people; Then whoever hears the sound of the trumpet, and takes not warning; his blood shall be upon his own head."* In verse 6, He says, *"But if the watchman sees the sword come, and blows not the trumpet, and the people are not warned; if the sword comes, and takes any person from among them, he is taken away in his iniquity; his blood will I require at the watchman's hand."* From this passage, it is clear that people must be warned of eternal destruction for the good of the people and the soul winner. Contrary to the opinion of many people, evangelism is not for the purpose of increasing the number of Church members but for the purpose of eternity.

There are two broad types of evangelism. They are personal and mass evangelism.

PERSONAL EVANGELISM

This is a person to a person, face to face dealing with an individual and presenting to him the message of salvation with the aim of winning him to the Lord. Because you are dealing with the person face to face, you can know the sex, age, level, outer appearance, facial expression and mannerism.

When we look at the faces of people, we see some smiling. We sometimes find it difficult to discover what they are going through. Hence they need the word of God to give them hope in this world, hope of eternity and a warning about what they should expect if they die as sinners.

One of the advantages of personal evangelism is that every Christian can reach out to people with the word of God. If a person just gives his life to Christ today, God can begin to use him immediately to reach out to others through personal evangelism. Even if he does not know how to preach, God can use his or her testimony to preach to people to come to Christ. The people he can reach include those who know his past life. God can reach and touch others through his testimony. It may not be possible for every Christian to be a preacher or teacher of spiritual things for these are gifts given by God. But there is no Christian however modest or insignificant he may see himself who is not appointed by the Lord to be a soul winner. In Mark 16:15, the Bible says, *"And he (Jesus) said unto them (All Christians), Go ye into all the world, and preach the gospel to every creature."*

Another advantage of personal evangelism is that it can be done anywhere. There are very few pulpits which had been occupied anyway but like Charles H. Spurgeon said, *"there are pulpits in every street and other places for personal evangelism."*

It is usually difficult to conduct Mass Evangelism in some places where there are crowds but it is possible to do personal evangelism everywhere.

Another advantage is that it can be done at anytime. The times of preaching services and Sunday schools are limited, but Personal Evangelism can be done seven days a week.

Personal Evangelism reaches all classes of people. There are people who cannot and who will not attend Church or religious services but through Personal Evangelism, they can be reached and often won to Christ.

We can also see that Personal Evangelism focuses attention on the individual. Preaching is necessarily general but Personal Evangelism is direct and personal.

Personal Evangelism provides large and far reaching results. For instance, if half of the Church members are zealous enough to be involved in Personal Evangelism and win a soul each month, there would be much more Church members before the end of the year than what the message within the Church would produce.

To qualify to be a soul winner, the person must be born-again. A person who has no life cannot give life. If he is really born-again, he would love to be involved in personal evangelism.

I remember my experience as a new convert. I am always concerned about where people will spend their eternity. So I tried as much as possible to reach out to so many people in the street, at home and even in the office. Even though this may surprise you a little, I must say here that the devil hates people who are involved in evangelism more than those who pray. The reason is that, by getting involved in evangelism, you are creating more enemies that will cause more trouble for the devil through prayers. Needless to say, evangelism is the mother of all Christian works. We can see that in the ministry of Jesus as He first reach out the first disciples in Matthew 4:18-22. In the whole of chapter 10 of Matthew, Jesus empowered the twelve disciples and sent them to reach out to lost souls.

All Christians who are involved in teaching, preaching, intercessory ministries came to Jesus Christ through the great commission called Evangelism.

METHOD OF PERSONAL EVANGELISM:

There are various methods that can be used in personal evangelism which can be invented, depending on the creativity of the soul winner. It is, however, important to consider some common and other methods that can be adopted by individual Christians under Personal Evangelism.

FACE TO FACE DISCUSSION PERSONAL EVANGELISM

This is the commonest method in personal evangelism. This may take any of these approaches: (i) direct approach (ii) indirect approach (iii) interrogative approach (iv) lifestyles approach and (v) doing a favour approach.

The Direct Approach: is the sudden introduction of the issue of eternity. Sometimes a stranger is met and may be asked of his relationship with God. His answer to such question will give the soul winner the opportunity to lead the stranger to Christ. Secondly, the soul winner should try as much as possible to deal with only one person at a time.

The approach can be applied if the time given to the soul winner is relatively short. It is going straight to the topic without any delay. In this case, questions about eternity can be asked. Questions like "does God really exist?" Or "is there really a place called hell or heaven?" may be used.

The Indirect Approach: always starts with subjects which may bear little or no relevance to the issue of Christianity and then graduate into spiritual things. This may require skills, especially if the person who is being addressed feels superior intellectually. In any case, the soul winner must avoid argument. A proverb says, argument spoils friendship.

127

Interrogative Approach: is a skillful way to arouse interest either through questions or other ways of getting the attention of the person the soul winner wants to lead the person for Christ. By using this method of approach, the soul winner is placing himself as a spiritual doctor who is trying to diagnose the spiritual state of the person he is dealing with before he knows how to minister to person. Hence he has to be tactful in the use of this method.

I went to visit a woman who sells some food items one day and met a young lady. When she was coming into the shop to buy some items, the woman told me the young lady was a prostitute that worked at a nearby hotel. She was so young and beautiful that I wondered how she got herself in a mess like prostitution. Then I decided to use interrogative approach to lead her to Christ. I first started by asking, 'do you know I love you?' She was happy to hear that, probably no one had said that to her before then. Her response encouraged me to press further, 'do you know there is someone who loves you much more than I do?' They were questions which I never border to get answers because I already got her attention. 'What if you think hell is not real and you discover it is real when you die?' At the end of the ministration, she completely handed her life over to Christ. She left prostitution to set up a restaurant business.

Lifestyle Approach: is using one's life to lead others to Christ. This approach must always be used by every true Christians. In 2 Corinthians 3:2, the Bible says, *'you are our epistle written in our hearts, known and read of all men.'* Here the Bible tells Christians that their conduct must reflect in their lives what they read in the word of God. Through their lifestyles, they can preach to individual person who reads them.

Doing A Favour Approach: as the name implies, it is leading a person to Christ by doing him a favour. When Christian does a favour to a person, he is showing love of Christ and also giving the person reason to follow the Jesus. I would illustrate this with the repeat of the story of a boy that went to preach to a starving family. When he got into the house, the family was starving. The soul winner who was just a teenager told the man he had come to tell the family about Jesus Christ. The man got so furious that he chased the boy out of the house. The boy did not give up. He went to his parents and asked them to give him some raw food items which he put inside a nylon bag. He went back to the family. The man looked more furious when he saw him again. The boy showed him the food items he had brought for the family, his countenance changed. He said, 'you're welcome!' The teenager used the food items to win the entire family over to Christ.

Having explained briefly the approaches that are common in face to face discussion method of Personal Evangelism, it is important for the soul winner to note the followings while dealing with a person.

The soul winner needs to understand the spiritual state of the person he is dealing with, probably through his response or attitude so that he may know how to lead him to Christ.

Secondly, the soul winner needs to constantly feed on the word of God so that he may be accurate in applying the word of God which is the most vital tool to lead anyone to Christ. The Bible says in 2 timothy 2:15, *'study to show thyself approved unto God, a workman that needed not to be ashamed, rightly living the word of truth.'*

The soul winner must communicate the message of the Lord in a simple and loving way without exhibiting 'holier than thou' attitude. Also he must not try to dominate the conversation. He needs to give the other person the chance to express himself. Through that, the soul winner can understand his condition and find a way to help him out of his spiritual problems. Do not be surprised if you discover that the attitudes of some Christians are the main reason a person does not want to accept Christ. Let him realize that everybody has his own life to account before God. God will not use the life of someone to judge anyone. He would use His Word to judge everyone.

The soul winner must not try in any way to attract attention to himself nor talk so much about himself. If there is need to share his personal testimony, he should do that in the way that will glorify God instead of attributing credits or pointing attention to himself. Many people are fond of attributing the glory of the Lord to themselves or their Church or their Pastor. I remember a man who was preaching on the air, telling people with problems to make sure they come to his Church to meet him for solutions. He shared the stories of how he prayed for people and how they got their miracles as if he was the one that solved their problems. We do not call that kind of preaching "kingdom evangelism." It is Church or self glory.

A soul winner must not give up or get discouraged if he fails to convert a person. He must not take offence even if he is insulted. There was a lady who was insulted for preaching in an open place. One of her listeners used her past promiscuous life to make her feel unworthy to preach the gospel. She did not mind the insults. She went to the same place over and over again, using her past to minister to the people since the people are conscious of it. God crowned her efforts and the sacrifice that seemed like shame with great success. She used the very thing people used to condemn her to preach to them.

Soul winning involves sacrifices in one form or the other. It can cost the soul winner his personal convenience or dignity or money or time or substances or even life. Whatever it is going to cost a soul winner to win souls for Christ, he or she must give it because it is an investment into the kingdom of God. No sacrifice is ever too much to make to win souls for Christ since the conversion of one person brings great joy to God in heaven (Luke 15:7). Besides, Jesus made the greatest of all sacrifices by dying for us. We must try to emulate Him in every way we can.

Another important thing a soul winner must bear in mind is that he is representing Jesus Christ who sends him to reach out to souls. So his or her attitude and appearance matter a lot. Many people have been driven away from Christ through the attitudes of some people who claim to be Christians. Some put off others with their ugly appearance or unnecessary doctrines.

A soul winner must learn to keep himself neat and tidy. He or she must get rid of his or her body or mouth odour and dirt that can easily put sinners away. A lady who could have easily reached out to me when I was swimming in sins came to me about twenty-five years ago. I didn't like the odour on her body. When she told me she had come to tell me about Jesus, I frowned at her. She misunderstood the expression on my face as a sign of pride. She found herself addressing the issue of pride. Actually, pride was not my problem. The issue was the odour coming from her body that put me off.

Most importantly, a soul winner must never forget to equip himself or herself with prayers and the word of God because he is involved in what the devil hate most - evangelism.

CORRESPONDENCE METHOD OF PERSONAL EVANGELISM

Letter writing and telephone calls including sending messages through mobile phones to one another is another of way of personal evangelism.

There was a testimony of a woman that proves that sending messages through mobile phones is very effective. While contemplating suicide, her friend who, from a far distance, sent text messages, telling her how God loves her. She also reminded her of the promises He had promised her, quoting the book of Deuteronomy 28. What particular touched her were the words, *"don't do anything funny to yourself but focus on Jesus for He is your only hope."* The message through the phone influenced her to change her mind. It gave her the strength to move on until she came into her blessing.

If you are led to send message to anyone through their phones, please, do not hesitate to do that. You can never tell how much it means to that person.

Letters including e-mails to friends, relatives and family can be used to talk about Christ to them. Because the people involved in the communication through letters or telephone calls are not strangers, it makes it a lot easier to share Jesus with each other. Every believer needs to use this method to tell friends, relatives, family and other acquaintance about Jesus.

MASS EVANGELISM

This is the method of evangelism that is used to reach out to a large number of people whether at the same or different times. Mass Evangelism can be compared with a fisherman who casts his net into the river with the aim of catching many fishes at the same time - various kinds - both small and big. Personal Evangelism on the other hand is like the same fisherman using a hook to catch one fish at a time. It is not every Christian that has the opportunity to be involved in Mass Evangelism but each of them has the opportunity to be involved in Personal Evangelism because we interact with other people everyday.

There are basically two means of Mass Evangelism which are crusade and media.

CRUSADE

Crusade in this context means attracting or gathering people together with the aim of sharing the Gospel with them. This can be done through various ways which include but not limited to the followings:

(i) Inviting people to the crusade ground, ministering to their spiritual and physical needs.

(ii) Using musical concert to attract people, using songs to share the word of God with them.

(iii) Organizing breakfast or dinner outreaches which people hear the word of God.

(iv) Sending people into the street or market to minister the word of God to the people.

(v) Using film shows / Drama to preach the word of God to the people. A group of Christians went to a village and took days to narrate the story of Jesus Christ to the villagers through drama presentations. At the end of the drama presentations, the entire villagers gave their lives to Jesus Christ.

Crusade is a very good method of Mass Evangelism, especially if it is backed with signs and wonders. I remember the time an Evangelist who went to the northern part of Nigeria, a place notable for so many fundamental Muslims at that time. The Evangelist delivered a very powerful message about Jesus Christ, saying, "Jesus is alive!" Unknown to him, many fanatical Muslims were so offended by the message that they took some weapons with them the following day, planning to kill the Evangelist. As he was speaking to the people, the Muslim fanatics raised up all sorts of weapons they have brought, telling him that he was a dead man unless he proves it to them that Jesus Christ is truly alive. The Evangelist looked at the people, smiled and then said, "don't crucify me yet. If Jesus does not prove himself, you can do whatever you like." Then he went ahead to preach more about Jesus, unmoved by their threats. As he was preaching, one of the leaders of the Muslim fanatics was struck by an invisible object and fell into a trance. He found himself in another place where he saw Jesus Christ, showing him the two hands that were nailed on cross. He said to the man, "I died for you. I was nailed on these hands because of you. Go and tell the people not to touch my servant."

When the man came to, he stood up, went to the platform and told the Evangelist that he was one of his enemies who just met Jesus. The man later told the people what he saw. The Evangelist told the man to ask Jesus to heal all the sick people in the place. The man said, "Jesus, if you are the one I saw, I want you to heal the sick people here." What followed was miracle galore. Before anyone knew it, several thousands of Muslims had been converted to Christianity.

It must be noted here that the work of evangelism is a great privilege and commission given to all Christians. God could decide to send his angels to do the work of evangelism but He desires to do it through Christians. Therefore, all Christians must be involved in it. One of the ways the Church and individuals can go about Mass Evangelism is through crusade that had been explained above. The other way is through media.

MEDIA

The influence of media is so great that there is urgent need for Christians to use it as means of Mass Evangelism. If they do not use it, the devil will continue to use it to destroy the works Christians are trying to do. One of the major tools the devil has used to bring the world and idolatry into the Church is media. To buttress this I would like to share with you what I experienced some years ago. I was walking down the street one day when I heard both children and parents saying some jargons. I thought it was a way the people normally amused themselves but when I heard the same jargons in about five other places, I became curious. I wanted to know the meaning and the source. I later found out that the jargons were actually uttered by an actor that was trying to interpret the role of a mad man on the television soap. Since that day I began to get more and more evidence that media can be very deadly tool the devil can use to lure the hearts of people from God and at the same time a very powerful means to win millions of souls for Christ.

In Ilorin, Nigeria where I began the ministry of communication of the word of God through publishing, seminar; film and media productions; I noticed that many fundamental Muslim families were converted to Christianity through media. Apart from the good news that was constantly preached on television, Christian TV soap always captivated the audience. The effect is always so great that the Muslims waged a serious war against Christian programs on television back then. The Bible says according to the Gospel of Saint Mark chapter 16 verse 15, *"and He (Jesus) said unto them (believers), Go you into all the world, and preach the gospel to every creature (both children and adults.)"*

We thank God for media which makes it possible for a minister to reach out to millions of people at the same or different times. But it is unfortunate that many Christians shy away from it, possibly because it is believed to be expensive. I do not believe the media is so expensive that Christians should be discouraged from using it. What each Christian needs to do is to find where he or she fits in. Some Christians may not have the grace to pull television audience but may have the grace to rally round and sponsor a Christian who has the grace to preach the Word of God through the media.

CLASSIFICATION OF MEDIA

We can classify media into three. These are (i) Print media/Publication (ii) Electronic Media (iii) Internet Media.

Print Media/Publication: This type of Mass Evangelism is done through magazines, newspaper, journals, books, tracts and other printed materials. Print media/publication is very easy and cheap means of mass evangelism. It is very flexible and potable. Unlike in electronics and internet media, no apparatus like television or radio or computer is required to communicate the message to receiver as long as he can read. The writer or the publisher of the word communicates directly to his audience and avoid the use of intermediary who at times can alter or add or remove some vital information as in the case of oral communication. Publications do not require visas to get out of the country and does not require invitation before it enters a well guarded place and preach the word of God. It repeats the same message all the time and at anywhere without changing or missing a word and without getting tired or bored. It moves rapidly and spread the news far and wide within a short time. The information in publication is preserved over the years as in the case of the Bible. It can talk to both poor and the rich whether they are in the street or in the jungle or other places.

I cannot help sharing the testimony of a man who was contemplating suicide when he was in a bus in Lagos, Nigeria. A tract titled, "After Death, What Next?" was given to another man who was walking down the street. The man angrily took the tract and threw it away. The tract went straight to the man in the bus. He picked it up and read it. God used the tract to save his life and add eternal life to it.

Publication is a vital tool in modern evangelism for these reasons:

(i) The Word of God can spread easily and quickly through it because it is fixable and portable. A man can get all he needs to know about God simply by reading the Bible without the need to go to a Bible school. Apart from that, more people are reached without any problem through publication. A group of people went for evangelism in an area and invited all the people they have met to come to the Church. While trying to find out if the people were really invited by the Church members, the Pastor requested the new converts to go to those who invited them. Many people could not find those who invited them but one of them who brought the tract with which he was able to trace the Church said, "whoever distributed this tract invited me." Some other people said similar things.

Since labourers, especially effective and dedicated ones are very few, publications are needed to compliment the efforts of Christians who are striving to minister to the people.

(ii) Evangelical Publishers do not face the problems of misinterpretations or information overload that are usually associated with oral communication in publications. Like the saying goes, a tale retold is a tale altered. Unlike the message from the pulpit which can be altered if it is retold to someone who is not present in the Church, with publication the same message that was preached years back can be recalled without missing any word. If the word of God had not been persevered through printed means, it would have been seriously altered as the years went by. It is the same word that was read by many generations we still read in modern days.

(iii) Publication does not take cognizance of readers' reaction to the message. A soul winner may be tempted to give up preaching to someone whose expression is intimidating. To illustrate this, I would like to share what I experienced many years ago. I met a group of youths in an area that was notable for violent drugs dealers. Many people avoided passing through that side for the fear of being attacked. Anyone going that way must first recite Psalm 23 which says, "The Lord is my Shepherd...Yea, though I walk through the valley of shadow of death..." As I was going through that way, one of the youths who knew I was a Pastor greeted me. I saw it as a good opportunity to share the word of God with them. I told the young man to call the rest together. As they all gave me their attention, I began to minister to them. "Save the sermon for your Church service!" They said in diverse ways. I did not give up but one of them who was smoking marijuana just blew the smoke of the stuff into my nose. I began to cough. Before I knew it, I had become the object of ridicule. The youths really had a nice time laughing at me as they blew more of the stuff to my face. I had to leave, coughing. It took me days before I recovered from the smoke. If I had given them tracts or any other printed material to preach to them, that would have save me the pain of facing those youths.

(iv) Publication can be a very cheap means of preaching to a large number of people and very easy means anyone, including new converts can use to propagate the Gospel. Sometimes, a Christian may find it very difficult, if not impossible to preach in an area but may find it easy to give the people around some tracts. Calvary Rock Resources is involved in writing and printing of various tracts and other publications for Churches. So we receive a lot of testimonies that really encourage us to invest in them and to encourage ministries to be involved in it. Even though it may look as if publishing the word of God is for some classes of people, I cannot overemphasis Its importance in evangelism. Some people who are given the tracts may not be able to read or may not be interested in reading the content but they can serve as the carriers of the message to those who would actually receive the word like in the case of the man that threw the tract given to him to the man who was contemplating suicide in the bus.

(v) As pointed out, publication repeats the same message without changing a word. It preaches the same the word over and over at anytime and anywhere without getting tired. There are so many other benefits or advantages of publications like portability, durability and flexibility which makes it unique and very vital in evangelism.

There are dangers in not using publications as means of evangelism. The dangers include the effect of ungodly publications that are destroying the moral values of the people. More and more people are getting initiated through publications, causing far more spiritual deaths than anyone can imagine. The devil is also using it to confuse many Christians. He goes as far as producing various publications and even perverted Bible in order to attack Christian faith.

Electronic Media: Evangelism through electronic media has to do with the use of radio or television or mobile phones. It also embraces anything that has to do with audio and audiovisual means. Materials like audio tapes, video tapes CDs DVDs are used to record messages, drama, music etc which are used for transmission on radio and tv.

Electronic Media has similar characteristics to that of print media and can be used also to spread the word of God in many areas. The differences between print and electronic media are in the use of apparatus like radio or television sets to pass the message as. While print media requires the ability to read, electronic media requires only the ability to see and or hear.

Internet Media: This is the latest technology among the three means of mass communication. It is a very easy and convenient way to reach out to the world. It has to do with network of computers around the globe, making the world a global village. Internet has covered so many areas of human lives, ranging from information, business, entertainment, education, politics and so many other things. The use of internet cannot be overemphasized as more and more things are coming up. Christians cannot afford to neglect this area because it saves them a lot of pain and struggle to reach out to the world. The internet had become a very destructive tool in the hands of the devil as he uses it to corrupt people, enlisting them as witches and wizards; members of secret cults, pornographic clubs_and all sorts of evil association you can imagine. Christians can use the internet to save souls rather than to watch and allow the devil to use it to lead people to hell. Christian organizations and individuals needs to use the internet to reach out to people.

In conclusion, it must be understood that there is no rigid form or way to reach out to souls. While some people can be reached through the means explained above, some can be reached through Personal Evangelism. In fact, the best form of evangelism still remains Personal Evangelism. Since most Christians are not really evangelizing, it becomes very crucial to use the various means of communications to evangelize and to teach the world the word of God. The most important thing in evangelism is love for souls and passion to win them for Christ. If we really love souls, we will do all we can to reach out to them for the Lord.

I pray that God will give us the heart and the wisdom to reach out to the souls that are heading to hell every minute. Amen!

CHECK OUT OTHER BOOKS BY DIPO TOBY ALAKIJA
Each Serves Either As Edifying Or Evangelical Or Missionary Or Academic Tool At Home, School, Bible Clubs, Sunday Schools, Church, Office And Other Fellowships

CHRISTIAN MINISTRIES AND BASIC LEADERSHIP
ISBN: 978-36348-7-9 ISBN: 978-978-36348-7-9
A Collection Of Resource Materials That Follows Up Successful Christianity And Basic Ministries Course Book

As it is common to say that the hood does not make a monk, the dignified positions and bogus titles of many Christian leaders in modern days do not really make them Gospel Ministers.

This course book - a compilation of five resource materials on Missions And Outreach Ministries, Christian Communication Arts, Christian Leadership, Christian Education Methodology and Ministries Of Improvisations - aims at making every matured Christian an effective minister and leader at their respective homes, communities and nations. It teaches various ways Christians can communicate the word of God, meeting up to their responsibilities as ministers and leaders that reconcile people to God, edifying the Body Of Christ and reaching out to souls at the same time.

All of the resource materials are in use in Bible Schools like College Of Christian Education And Missions, in Churches and other ministries to raise Christian workers, Evangelists, Missionaries and other Ministers that serve at various levels and leadership capacities.

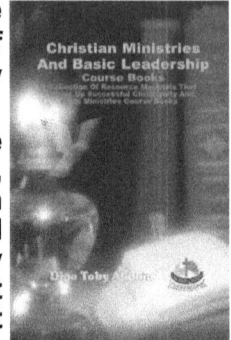

FOOTSTEPS IN THE MUD
ISBN: 978-36348-9-5 ISBN: 978-978-36348-9-3
The Drama Package Of Results Of Research Works That trace Global And Societal Vices To The Corrupt Or Lost Of Family Values

The 13-Episode drama book involves Bosede who learnt many wrong things from her parents' conduct and foul language. She was forced to marry Kola when she became pregnant. Using her mother's method to handle her father, she tried to subject Kola to her control. In the course of that, she made life terrible for him. Although her mother tried to warn her of the implications of maltreating her husband but Bosede has grown out of control. Consequently, while looking for peace, Kola was pushed out of the house. He made friends with some guys who taught him the unholy ways of life and influenced him to become a menace in the house.

Junior who was born at time the couple never proved to be responsible parents also learnt wrong things from them.

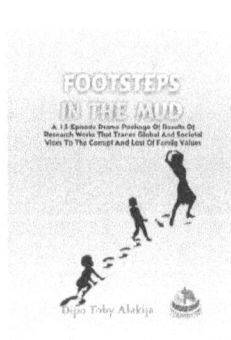

138

He decided to follow his father's footsteps by taking alcohol when he was in primary school. As if that was not bad enough, he tried to teach other children in the school the madness in his home. A school teacher, however, was able to influence him and his mother by teaching them Christian morals. Even then, Junior was soon caught in the crossfire at home as his father tried to enlist him as a future member of a secret cult that posed as a social club.

INSANITY OF HUMANITY
ISBN: 978-36348-6-0 ISBN: 978-978-36348-6-2
The Results Of Research Works Into Various Methods Of Brainwashing

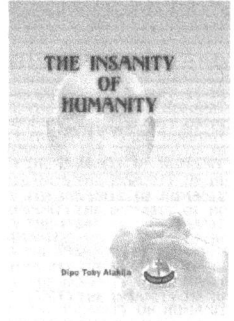

Man is made to exercise his freewill. The mind of his own and the power to choose between right and wrong, good and evil, light and darkness is about to be washed away through brainwashing. The agents of control dubbed as Secret Government by John Todd (the top Illuninati defector) have put necessary machinery in place to ensure that all human beings are in conformity in their thinking and ways of life, trying to wipe away diversity, which makes each person unique.

This book attempts to shed light on how the techniques of mind control are applied through the use of propaganda, education, entertainments, drugs, religions, media and other means of communications. It is the result of research works, some of which are based on findings of various researchers and writers like Bugger Lugz, Edward Hunter, Hadley Cantril, Herbert Krugman, David L. Robb, Vaughan Bell, Juliana Gomez, Ryan Duffy Vice, Henry Makow, David Nicholls, Fritz Springmeire, Steven Hassan, Renate Thienel, Debra Pursell, Mary Pride and a host of others who are acknowledged in this book.

NO MORE TEARS TO SHED
ISBN: 978-49874-3-0 ISBN: 978-978-74-3-1

Kidnappers took Tokunbo away from his grand parents in a city in Nigeria when he was a little boy. A nice woman found him in another town and gave him a false identity. She spoilt him with love, making him to grow into a rebellious teenager that was not appreciated anywhere. When Janet made him a Christian, however, life began to make sense to him until the day he was beaten to the point of death for the offence he knew nothing about. He left the town for the city which, unknown to him, held his true identity and the link to his parents in the United States. To find them was only a question of time.

THE UNROMANTIC LOVE BIRDS
ISBN: 978-49847-5-7 ISBN: 978-978-4974-5-5
And other short stories about love and marriages

They were very much in love right from their school days but when they got married and had children, romance became the game Charles' wife refused to play. No matter how much he tried to make her understand the unbearable condition her unromantic attitude has subjected him into, she would not change. Consequently, after enduring for so long, he was forced to look for the women that would make up for her weakness. He unofficially married a beautiful lady of insane jealousy. Though she was ready to give him what was missing in his marriage, it soon dawn on him that he has solved one big problem only to create a bigger one.

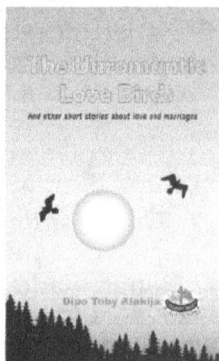

THE BATTLE OF THE CONQUERORS
ISBN: 978-49874-7-3 ISBN: ISBN: 978-978-49874-0-7-9

Wickedness takes over the land of Bondage from First Couple and subjects everybody into slavery without giving anybody the chance to be free. Love brings The Redeemer from Eternity and offers the slaves the chance to escape. Wickedness soon declares war and engages everyone in the battle. The Redeemer makes the redeemed people Conquerors by giving them the armour of war and Comforter but Wickedness cannot be undone. He has several thousands of years of experience in the war. So he is quick to recognize the weakness of the redeemed people who are ignorant of their strengths and advantages. Although the Conquerors fight like immutable giants, rescuing victims of war, many people suffer heavy casualties.

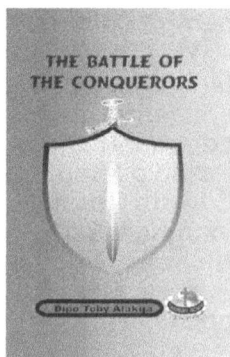

Since King Wickedness knows that a redeemed person is strong enough to chase one thousand of his warriors at a time, and two would put ten thousand into flight, he enlists as one of his warriors the people's deadliest enemy called Disunity.

Wickedness is able to strike the people by making them to fight with one another, turning what is supposed to be their best moments in the battle into tales of woes.

BLOODSHED IN CAMPUS
ISBN: 978-07350-3-8 ISBN: 978-978-07350-3-6

A poor widow tearfully warned her son, Richard, against joining the bad wagon when he got an admission into one of the Nigerian Universities. He resisted the membership of groups of students, including the Christian Fellowship until he had an encounter with a member of The Black Skulls - a deadly and ruthless secret cult on the campus.

Before Richard knew what he was up against, the head of The Black Skulls had arranged items for his initiation into the cult. While resisting being initiated, he ran to the Christian Fellowship for help. The leader of the Christian Fellowship dragged The President of Students' Union Government (S.U.G) into the conflict. With the involvement of the S.U.G President, another formidable cult called The Red Eyes felt obliged to team up against The Black Skulls. Then the campus turned into a battlefield and BLOODSHED became the order of the black day.

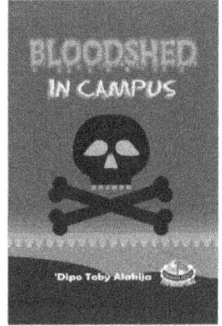

NETWORK BIBLE CLUB
YOUTH AND ADULT BOOK ONE
ISBN: 978 - 978- 49874-9-X ISBN: 978-978-49874-9-3
A collection of 26 life transforming stories, 26 poems, 26 hymn tuned songs and weekly Bible lessons

The issue of moral instructions in schools and at homes is threatened with extinction. Consequently, so many youths are involved in prostitution, drug addictions, cultism, fraudulent practices, armed robberies and other crimes. Those who are supposed to be trained as leaders in various walks of life are the ones posing serious threats to many lives. Many parents who fail to add moral values to the upbringing of their children often times breed potential criminals under their roofs without knowing it. Apart from these, many other people negatively influence young ones through the media, music, publications, films, conduct and foul language; making them to lose their moral and family values.

This book one just like the rest of other volumes is an attempt to bring back moral instructions into schools and campuses through the use of stories, hymn tuned songs, poems, Bible lessons and class activities. It is designed to assist teachers and ministers in Secondary Schools, Bible Clubs, Churches and Campus Fellowships to teach people, especially youths the Word of God and serves as a school text book in subjects relating to literature, music and other creative works.

FOUNDATION BIBLE CLUB A-Z STORY BOOK
ISBN: 978-49874-2-2 ISBN: 978-978-49874-2-4
Volume 1 With 26 Stories, 26 Bible Lessons, 26 Rhymes And 26 Songs For Book For Young Minds

An adage says, "a man who builds a house without building his child builds what the child will later sell." Proverbs 22:6 says, "train up a child in the way he should go: and when he is old, he will not depart from it." This book is an attempt to assist parents and teachers to meet up to the challenges that befall them in carrying out this important function in the light of the moral decadence that is prevailing all over the world.

The first edition of the book was used by several thousands of teachers, ministers and parents in schools, Churches and homes to build the moral values of young ones. Apart from the stories, songs and Bible passages for the young ones to study, there is a seminar material that is based on the lecture which the author delivered to school proprietors, children ministers and Christian professionals in this volume.

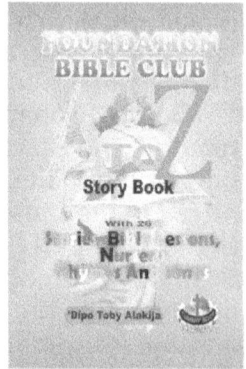

RANSOM FOR LOVE
ISBN: 978-49874-8-1 ISBN: 978-978-4987-4-8-6

She accepted his marriage proposal without knowing the kind of person he was. She soon discovered that he was a mean and ruthless guy who was always ready to get whatever he wanted by all means even if he has to pay for it with the lives of others. She was in his bondage, especially when her parents who believed he was a generous and gentleman were on his side.

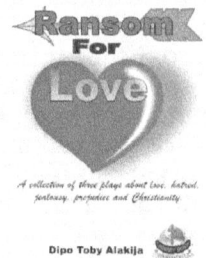

Because she considered the proposal to marry him as a marriage engagement with the devil incarnate, she decided that she would rather die than to share her life with him. Then out of the blues, this passionate gentleman sneaked into her life despite all she did to discourage him. She could not resist his love for her when he offered to set her free from the devil incarnate. Then the battle began – sooner than they anticipated.

THE WEIGHT OF DEATH
ISBN: 9978-36348-0-1 ISBN: 978-978-36348-0-0
(Story Of The Spirit Eyes Series)
PLAY ONE: HORROR IN THE FAMILY: Talimi probably did not

envisage his death when he was trying to compel his son, Damola to succeed him in the occult Brotherhood. Other members of the secret cult were aware of the battle between them. So when Talimi died; his family, especially Damola who was a diehard Christian began to fall prey to the cult. Using all their powers and the spirit that posed as Talimi's ghost, the cult waged war against the family, tormenting and making them to be at loggerheads.

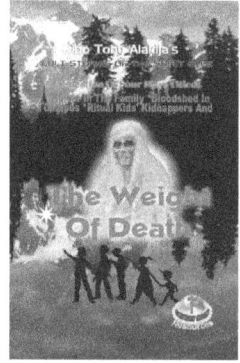

PLAY TWO: RITUAL KIDS' KIDNAPPERS: Victor and the rest of the members of the School Bible Club were taught that there are lots of evil people in this world but he did not understand why God allowed him to be among the children that were taken away from their parents. He soon understood that he was to be used by God to rescue other children who did not know that everyone that truly believes in Jesus has the power to overcome evil.

PLAY THREE: THE WEIGHT OF DEATH: Awoseun would not have known the real source of problems of mankind if his father had not given him the power to see demons tormenting the people in different ways. What he was yet to know, however, was the power of light over darkness. When he was caught in crossfire between these powers, he desperately sought for deliverance.

CALVARY ROCK RESOURCE BOOKLETS
ISSN: 1595 93X
The Quarterly Missionary Booklets That Are Designed To Teach Children, Youths And Adults In Schools, Fellowships, Churches, At Homes, Office And Other Places.

Although all the various volumes of this booklet can be used independently of other books but it is recommended that it should be used as part of supplementary materials to make up for Foundation and Network Bible Club Story Books for both children and adults in School, Church, Campus, Office and other Fellowships.

Each of the volume is rich with quarterly Bible lessons, stories, drama, songs, seminar, tract materials and a host of other things that can be used to edify, educate, entertains and evangelize every category of people, ranging from children to elderly persons.

Every volume is designed to equip school teachers, ministers in Churches or campus or office fellowships and other people who wish to work with the Lord.

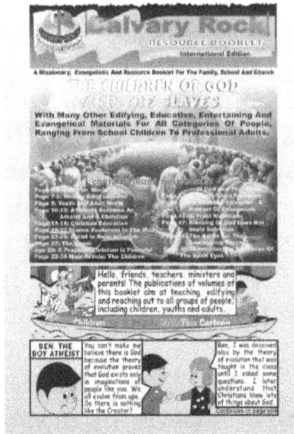

All These And Other Books Are Distributed Worldwide And Published By The Publishing House Of Calvary Rock Resources

*Ikenne-Remo, Nigeria
*Manchester, United Kingdom
*New York, United States

www.calvaryrock.org

www.ingramcontent.com/pod-product-compliance
Lightning Source LLC
LaVergne TN
LVHW051642080426
835511LV00016B/2436